NUTRiGlamorous

How to Feel Beautiful Inside and Out

Halle Eavelyn

Gratitudes

Bryn Austin, Tamika Auwai, Sandy Babin, Kim Coles, Tyler Ellison, Rebecca Hahn, Tracette Hillman, Anya Randall, Judith & Don Schecter, you all know how you helped and I'm so grateful

Contents

"Love yourself first, and everything else falls into line. You really have to love yourself to get anything done in this world."

— Lucille Ball

Intro

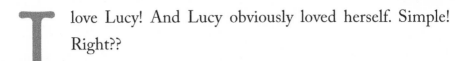

I love Lucy! And Lucy obviously loved herself. Simple! Right??

It's just... simple and easy are not the same thing at all.

If they were, you wouldn't be reading this book.

Today, we women are no longer the eye-rolling housewives of Lucille Ball's era. We are CEO's. We're mamas. We're pioneers, innovators, caregivers, entrepreneurs, powerhouses—we're also not quite *there* yet, and... we're working on it.

Our lives are so full, and we feel so thankful—it's just... GOOD GODDESS! It's tough to love ourselves when we're spread like mayo across a million obligations.

Exhausted from work, depressed because of world events, fed up with all the "everyone else" and not enough YOU in your life, pooped from hiding from the little nudge that tells you you're not doing it right (even though it looks to the world like you are), feeling the clock ticking down...

The truth is, we feel like we are never doing, or being, enough.

Sure, you've accomplished so much, in every walk of life, yet there's one checkbox on the To Do list that stays empty, booted to the next day, then the next... forever uncompleted (there's NOTHING worse than a box on the To Do list left unchecked, right?)

If you feel a little unhappy, and don't know why…

If you can't get your diet together, or exercise more than once a month, if you daydream about finding just five more minutes…

If you feel disconnected, unfulfilled or just 'cloudy'…

Your To Do list isn't finished!

There's only one thing left, and getting it done will help everything else fall into place. It's something you've needed to do for a long time. The problem is, nobody ever taught you how to do it. And in this modern world, your unique life, with the challenges only you face—it's something no one could have prepared you for anyway. It's a journey you have to face gloriously, confidently, joyfully on your own.

It's *taking care of yourself so you can take care of every piece of your world.*

Or, what we call becoming (ta-da!) NutriGlamorous.

It's all about you

"Hey, I follow hashtag selfcare on Instagram!"

"I tried minimalism!"

"I have a green smoothie sometimes, and I even try to take five minutes for myself... nearly every day."

And I'm here to tell you—before we say anything else—you are doing wonderfully.

So what's missing? Why do you feel like you're never enough?

You tell yourself to "get it together!" (or that's what you hear from others, kindly or sometimes not so much). Eventually,

it becomes a hill you can never climb. You "should" yourself until you feel like you are just never good enough.

How can you pull your career together if your business isn't going well, or you are at a job you truly hate, or that isn't even a stepping stone to your big dream? Or if you're barely making ends meet?

How can you eat healthy when organic food is so expensive, cooking is a chore and yo-yo dieting left you with an actual fear of bread? Or it seems like something sweet is the only thing you can look forward to after a long, hard day?

Is it possible to have a wonderful home, great kids, a partner who loves you (and you love right back) and a fulfilled career, all without feeling like you need 29 hours every day?

You are a unique person (just like everyone else), so how can anyone else show you how to

Get

YOURSELF

Together?

This book will show you exactly how. It doesn't give you a 1–2–3 solution; it's not a box you have to fit into (here's a secret: there is no box). It's a map, full of all the different paths you can take to plan your own journey, stop at the

sights you want to see on the way, and avoid boredom on routes that don't work for you.

If you're like me, and you've read it all, seen it all, and even done it all, then I encourage you to read with new eyes, to keep your mind open as you read. The two most dangerous words in the English language are "I know." Why? Because there's a big difference between knowing and KNOWING. The root word *know* comes from the Greek, *gnosis*, which the dictionary defines as "knowledge of spiritual mysteries." So when your brain wants to helpfully remind you that you

have already read this concept or done that exercise, just say, "Thank you for sharing" and keep going.

"Thank you for sharing" is one of the most powerful phrases ever; though it's amazingly simple, don't let that fool you. If *simple* and *easy* were the same thing, you'd already be as healthy and as happy as you desire. When you say, "Thank you for sharing," your brain can suddenly feel heard — which it has not before since you (like almost all people) are probably in resistance all the time.

Think about it: you read it, and your brain tells you "Been there, done that, got the T-shirt." Now you resist that information because you know it intellectually. Yet if you were already doing it, you would be on your way to achieving that goal already. You have just thrown up a barrier that "protects" you from doing the very thing that would help.

Why? Because our brains want us to stay stuck. Stuck = safe, according to your brain. And safe is where we don't have to step out into the danger zone of being seen or heard in a way where we might shine too brightly and scare everyone around us with our new way of living.

If you're going to be NutriGlamorous, you might have to step out of your comfort zone and act in a new way that makes your brain afraid of you failing. It will protect you with those two ultra-dangerous words, *I know.* Take your pick. You can keep

going the way you have been, safe and stuck, or you can tell your brain, "thank you for sharing" and rock on with your new self. Luckily, "life begins at the end of your comfort zone," right?

Bumper sticker philosophy is simple because it's accurate and easy to remember. Simply keep reading and KNOWING and soon you'll be living the life of your dreams.

What is NutriGlamorous?

NutriGlamorous is the word we use to describe Glammers: ageless women who are truly healthy, happy, beautiful and fulfilled—for themselves, not for others.

Kindness is good, and needed more than ever—and you, lady, have probably been raised not to be selfish, to be kind and good always. Generosity is awesome. It's just we've taken it to an extreme. It's hard to love yourself right now in modern society; if it were easier, the world would be a nicer, kinder place.

Unfortunately, that's the problem.

Selfishness is essential. Now, before you drop this book like a bad first date, shaking your head at how the silly author clearly doesn't understand, let me explain. Putting yourself first is seen as undesirable, unfeeling—and sometimes plain impossible. Just explain to me how, if you don't take care

of yourself first, will you have anything left to give others? If you're not happy, well-cared-for and motivated, how can you do what you were put on this Earth to do?

The world will get out of your way, I promise. If there is no way for you to believe this or be OK with it, think of it in this new way: when you tend your own garden first, you have more harvest to share with everyone. You also want to weed that garden often; more on that later.

This book is your flight attendant on a new trip through life: fasten your seatbelt, pull on your own oxygen mask, and get ready for some subtle shifts that will change everything and make you a whole heck of a lot happier along the way.

Being a Glammer is learning how to stop asking, and start taking in a new way—with grace, love, and dignity. How to reclaim the time and energy you need to move mountains, instead of waiting for the stars to align.

Nutrition: It's about feeding yourself with the best of nature's abundance, inside and out, because you deserve it.

Glamorous: It's about discovering your own style, appreciating others' without being pressured to copy, rejecting dumb trends and being confident, timeless, and happy with who you are.

Nutrition + Glamorous = NutriGlamorous: the Art of Being Perfectly YOU.

About this book

As I said, this book is not exactly by-the-numbers plan for success—there's no diet here (ok, there are several), no required exercise regime to follow (that's here too if you want it), no daily tasks (unless you want them) or twelve-step solution (and I love me some 12-step!) In other words, it's for YOU to decide what's right for you, from real, authentic advice distilled from the collective experiences of this woman and countless others, on how to create your own solution easily.

You can read all the chapters in order or skip ahead to the subject that interests you most. You won't be missing out; they're written to be read independently when you need a dive into one topic, or digested as a whole.

It's all here for you — just keep an open mind and remember some things will naturally spark your inner guidance. Those are the ideas you want to reach for first and implement before the others.

Beautycons

Do you follow those profiles on Instagram?

Women with great bodies leading great lives, having a great time (the ones that make you think... WHY isn't that me??)

Some of them do yoga on the beach, eat colorful rainbow vegan buddha bowls and practice mindfulness.

Others revel in the latest styles, flaunting curves and toned arms in sultry poses at hipster locales with hundreds of influential friends.

Or maybe you follow the ones who live on a farm, grow their own organic produce and find the time to weave baskets, raise kids and still enjoy hot turmeric tea by the wood burner on TV-free nights.

None of them seem like Beautycons—yet... It depends on one simple thing: are they living their true, authentic lives? Or is it just a performance for likes and follows?

If they post impossibly beautiful photos, and don't acknowledge that their lives behind the scenes are messy, imperfect, and that they're sometimes sad or lonely like everyone else... Beautycon alert!

Beautycons view social media as a lens they can use to magnify their own self-importance; oh, and they're everywhere in real life, too.

They're the mean girls who never wanted to sit near you in school, though they seem plenty friendly now (and freak you out by pretending that they always liked you).

They might have married for shallow reasons, and now vent their frustrations by pointing out what's wrong with everyone else in a Miss Judgy McJudgyPants way.

If they preach kindness and tolerance and then proceed to gossip about everyone around them, DING DING!!

They may be the cosmetic surgeries, tattoos, designer clothes and gym memberships, rock climbing, Hamptons or yoga retreats people all around us... going and doing, not because it makes them happy, just so they can take a selfie and everyone else can be jelly watching them live their perfect lives.

They lie about their lives and happiness levels to make you think they have it all. Beautycons don't ask for help, help you achieve your goals or understand kindness—they complain, drag you down and do good things for show. It's not bad manners, or terrible intentions — it's all just FOMO (fear of missing out) or just plain fear. As I like to say, "Everyone's always doing their best — it's just sometimes that SUCKS." Welcome to the Beautycons of the world.

And, you want to know something really interesting?

Authenticity, honesty and vulnerability are becoming trendy. With more celebrities preaching mindfulness, being true to yourself and embracing what's real, it can be tough to tell who's really NutriGlam—and who's doing it to sell their new product line. ("I steam my vag, and so should you!")

It's easy to fall into a negative cycle of wanting to please others—we've all made those mistakes. Instead of calling out the Beautycons or hoping they will fall in line with your beliefs, smile and let them continue their journey; they'll figure it out. Choose the path that's best for you. You do you, as the kids say.

And hey, if this piece resonates with you a little too much — don't worry; you're reading this book and you get to make some new decisions!

How to be a Glammer

In this book you'll find advice on many core areas of your life: eating, moving, loving, breathing, giving and more. You'll discover all the ways you can invite joy into your life and kickstart your own natural path to becoming truly NutriGlamorous.

Just remember, as with any worthwhile pursuit — it's not the destination, it's your experience on the way there! Becoming NutriGlam means revealing more of what's become hidden over long, stressful years taking care of others, climbing the career ladder and following unproductive choices.

It begins here, with this book. Enjoy the journey...

"And the day came when the risk to remain tight in a bud was more painful than the risk it took to blossom"

— Anaïs Nin

Core

1

Let's talk about who we are as people, and how we show up. Imagine that you are looking at a huge cliff in Hawaii, and a waterfall has been running down that same cliffside for millions of years. It's worn these giant grooves into the side of the cliff where the water comes down in the same place—day after day, week after week, year after year.

We have these same pathways that our brains create. So when you think a certain way over a period of time, your brain wants to react the SAME WAY every time. You have to choose to make changes (like the ones in this book) and then you have to create a deliberate awareness of the thing you want to change each time so that your behavior is different.

You're going to talk about becoming a Glammer, or you're going to think about it, and you're going to share with the people you love, care about, or at least hang out with. And they're going to say, "That's stupid. That won't work. Why do I care?" And you're going to think, "Well, it seemed like a good idea, it's just these are the people I have to spend all my time with," and then you're going to stay stuck in the same patterns you're in.

So my question for you, is, how is what you are doing right now working for you? How are your habits serving you? Are you getting everything that you want out of life?

Are you on that hamster wheel every day and not enjoying your work as much as you would like to, or not enjoying your life as much as you would like to? Well, all those people who are saying that this new information is not important have that same problem; they're not that happy and they want to keep you down there with them. The difference is that they are not reading these words, and you are.

The core question is, what are you going to do with tomorrow? And the next tomorrow? And all the rest of the days of your life, long or short?

The author of *Secrets of the Millionaire Mind*, T. Harv Ecker, asks, "If you knew that you had to make $1 million this year, could you?" Most people say no. Now the question becomes, "If you had to make $1 million this year or your family would be killed and so would you, could you?" Though that may sound drastic, it's all just a matter of degrees. How important is your big goal?

How does this apply to you? You'll make $1 million, or you won't. It's not about the money; I am suggesting that you consider that your life can change IF YOU WANT IT ENOUGH.

Whether you believe it or not, fear is the only thing holding you, me, all of us, back.

When I was twenty-two years old, I left the theater to start my own software business with three partners. It was the year before CD-ROMs came out (I know, I'm dating myself — CD-ROMs were after vinyl records and before DVDs). We knew absolutely nothing, and we were probably going to fail. Most people that knew anything about business told us that. Luckily, we knew nothing about business. We only knew that we had an idea we wanted to show the world. We acted without fear, and we were a tremendous success.

You may think that you don't have enough money, you don't have enough time, you don't have enough skills, you're not

smart enough, etc. If you think that, someone has probably told you, at least once, every one of the things that you don't have enough of to accomplish your dream or your goal. At the core, those are Beautycon lies. This book has all the answers to make sure you can stop buying into them.

Forgive whoever told you those lies. Forgive yourself for listening, for making that story your reality. If you don't feel like you can do that, if it doesn't feel safe, remember that forgive and forget are NOT the same thing. You don't have to forget, and you don't have to make the same mistakes, ever again.

And... it's your choice. You can stay exactly where you are, for as long as you like. It's just that you're being called to something greater. You can tell because you are reading this book, and not watching reruns of *The Real Housewives of New Jersey*.

Simply tell the Universe what you want, and for once, don't ask "how?" If you can get out of your own way, you will be able to accomplish the thing you are afraid you can't. Even if you only have five minutes today on the potty to get it done. That's how I wrote my first book, by the way... on the toilet, five minutes a day. We can accomplish any change in small enough increments, Glammer, and this is your chance to do just that.

Over a hundred years ago, the French philosopher Pierre Teilhard de Chardin noted: "We are not human beings having a spiritual experience. We are spiritual beings having a human experience."

This is your opportunity to step into that. Don't miss out. The best part is, once you start on the path, you can keep going just by asking, "What's the next smallest step that I can take?" You don't need to know HOW right up front. Just see your goal, your desire, and keep asking that question. Then let signs and inspiration guide you to the that next step.

On my journey to become NutriGlamorous, I've traveled all over the world and experienced spirituality in all the places and cultures I've been to. In fact, I kind of collect spiritual experiences everywhere I go. I collect stories about the world coming together to orchestrate my highest and best good or that of those around me.

Several years ago, I was in Bali, and I had a HUGE up-leveling around love, right in the middle of the tenth *Eat Pray Love* tour I was leading. This experience caused me to leave my partner of nearly twenty-five years, who I thought was my soulmate, and embark on a whole new chapter of my life. I didn't know it at the time, yet it was an enormous push towards something I had asked for deliberately. I had

told the Universe I wanted to be more authentically ME, to live my truth with a capital T. And the Universe, about three months later, delivered an amazing solution that I could never have created for myself.

I was so scared at first — I couldn't see a step in front of me — I could barely see a half-step. And I kept trusting Spirit to guide me. Whenever I was afraid, I would just say, "I TRUST." Because I couldn't even see a little of what I needed to be, or where I needed to go, for about a year.

Then, as I sat down in front of the amazing and majestic Victoria Falls in Zambia, I asked Spirit if it had a message for me. And I could feel, like puzzle pieces falling into place over my head, that my time of fear, or blind faith, was ended. That my direction was clear and that my decision to change my comfortable world was the right one — that the joys and riches of the world that awaited me were so much bigger than I could have imagined.

I want that for YOU, Glammer. I want you to know the joy of living the life you were born to live, not slogging through life with hopes and dreams buried in the back of your mind to be pulled out at three in the morning when you can't sleep.

My question to you is, are you just watching? Are you just reading? Or are you implementing? Are you making the changes of the experiences that you are hearing about? Are

you making the changes of the opportunities that you are being invited to?

Because, look, here's the deal. We are always being called to something greater. We are all, always, being called to something greater. Right now, I am living the very best moments of my life. They are the very best because they are the ones I am the most aware of, the most excited about. The biggest opportunities I've got are in front of me, even though

I am officially middle-aged. I am not a young thing with my entire life ahead of me. Yet, I really am. And so are you. This day, this very minute, this now. It's everything. It's the first to-be-lived moment of the rest of your life.

Start from that core. And keep reading.

"The food you eat can be either the safest and most powerful form of medicine or the slowest form of poison."

— Ann Wigmore

Eat 2

What we eat sustains us. It fuels our bodies and often our social connections and emotional wellbeing, too — food as entertainment, food to soothe, food as art, food as love.

Unfortunately, for many women, the simple act of eating food has become a huge source of pressure, stress and doubt. We are constantly bombarded with media and advertisements telling us the "right" way to look, weigh and be happy is only possible through strict dieting and an absence of fun. That couldn't be further from the truth!

Whether you've been a foodie all your life or you're just now learning that quinoa is pronounced "KEEN-whah" (as in, "Whah' the heck is that?") a world of healthy, delicious eating options is waiting inside every supermarket, restaurant, and corner store. Done right, eating gives us energy, makes us glow, and connects us with the earth and the people around us.

Time to rediscover good eating.

How to create a diet

The word "diet" basically means "the way you eat." The word DIET has gotten fraught with weight, literally and figuratively. Detached from all that we have overlaid, it's just food.

There are six key questions [1] to consider when designing your personal diet:

1. How many meals do you prefer to eat each day?

2. Do you like to cook?

3. Do you need support for your diet?

4. Do you LOVE to dine out?

5. Have you allocated for daily treats if that's important for you?

6. How much exercise are you planning to get?

The answers to these questions will help you figure out what your body needs, as well as what your taste buds are interested in.

For example, some people stick to a strict three meals a day, while others are grazers who prefer to nibble throughout the day (think cows with grass) and leave less room for a sit-down experience. (Which might not stop you from eating three meals a day on top of that, which is why you might need to examine your habits from the ground up.) Others subsist on just one or two large meals, which may illogically cause them to gain weight, too. Back to basics: start noticing where your routine and preferences take you, and then divide your calories accordingly.

When you create a diet, you will need to make changes that you might not expect. Having a solid support network is one way to make that transition smoother. How much has to change in your environment and social habits to accommodate a new eating plan? When you have friends to cheer you on and clean, empty kitchen cupboards at home — rejoice!

Otherwise, get some help, girl — a support group, an online meal planner with affirmations, something. Just remember, once your initial enthusiasm wears off, you know your husband stashed Cheetos in the pantry and everyone at work is having birthday cake, a solid support network will be vital to fall back on.

The answers to these six questions need to be honest. In the next chapter, we'll discuss incorporating more joyous movement into your life. Meanwhile, it's important to be honest with yourself about what you can reasonably expect to achieve. Experts recommend at least thirty minutes a day of moderate physical activity, like walking or riding a bike, as often as you can. However, you may have to build up to that, especially if your current routine isn't very physically active.

One last note before we dive in! Before you start any diet or exercise routine that is a drastic change for your body, it's important to consult your doctor. Though you know your body best, your doctor can help you determine your body's nutritional needs.

Dieting

If you're a Glammer who's ever been on a diet, you know just how much of your own power you've given over to food. According to Judy Mahle Lutter, in her book *The Bodywise Woman*, up to fifty percent of women are "on a diet" at any given time. For teenagers, this number jumps up to ninety percent, and up to fifty percent of younger kids have tried a diet at some point—which is really sad and has just been getting worse over the years.

A friend posted her kids' back-to-school pics, with her son and daughter showing all the stats on chalkboards they held up. Looking at the ten-year-old boy and the eight-year-old girl's photos side by side, I noticed a subtle distinction. While the boy proudly displayed his height and weight, the girl had artfully covered hers with her hand. This perfectly beautiful, perfectly proportional young lady was already being taught to be ashamed of her body by our society. At eight. What the H-E-double-toothpicks is wrong with us?

If you're unhappy with your body, maybe it's your eyes that are broken. If your doctor, your scale, and your clothing are all telling you something different than your mirror, maybe you need to consider that somewhere along the way you developed a flawed sense of what physically attractive means.

There is a difference between having fat and being fat. There is a difference between being fat and being unhealthy. There are big, gorgeous dancers, yoginis, even Zumba instructors… and maybe it's no accident they always look like they are having a great time!

If you've dieted, what were the results? Did you struggle to shed pounds? Or if you dropped the weight, did it leave you unhappier than you thought you'd be? Or — worst nightmare ever — did you lose weight, only to watch the scale creep back up as soon as you stopped your strict diet?

Many of us are guilty of "rubber-banding" our diets. We go months or years on autopilot, eating what we want, whenever we want. All of a sudden, we decide, "This is it! Today is the day! I'm going to commit to the Medi-Keto-Vegan-Pesca-Beach-Weight Diet!" And for a few days or weeks, we do. Until that first plate of cheat nachos threatens our resolve, when we snap right back into bad habits.

It doesn't feel great. In fact, this unhealthy relationship with dieting is often what gives women an unhealthy relationship with their food.

If you took steps towards becoming a healthier, happier version of you, you DEFINITELY didn't fail. Maybe just sit with that for a bit. You succeeded because you made the effort, even if you didn't reach the goal.

We beat ourselves up instead of taking a closer look at what we *should* be studying: what went wrong.

If you're not going to *enjoy* a diet, you're not going to get results. So, ask yourself:

- **Were my options too limited?** If the answer is yes, that diet wasn't the right one for you. It's important to *like* the food you put in your body, not just tolerate it.

- **Did I lack willpower?** If you felt like you never had any self-control, that feeling may have been from a lack of self-care. Checking in with yourself at every step of the journey is key to healthy, nutritious eating.

- **Do I need to change my environment altogether, and give my self-control a break?** When in doubt, throw it out! When you start a new diet, you need to equip yourself with the right home base and toolkit. That means no ice cream hiding in the back corner of the freezer and, instead of empty calories waiting for you at home, empty cabinets waiting for a new stock of healthy staples.

Remember: food is just one of many ways we can give ourselves love every day.

Dieting in the traditional sense is not self-love. For many women, it can feel like punishment, especially when you tack

on a time limit. Whether it's a 3-day juice cleanse, a 14-day I-have-to-fit-into-my-reunion-dress diet, the 30-day transformation or a 90-days-to-the-wedding overhaul, they all are set up to say that you can eventually go back to the old ways. Even if those diets tell you that you'll 'break old habits' and 'forge new relationships with food' so you stay svelte after the program is over, a deadline (while great for marketing) tells you the subtle lie that you only have to put up with it for so long.

Let's try a thought exercise: imagine a diet that got you to your goal weight, made you feel great, and gave you tons of energy. The kicker? You're only allowed to eat carrots for the rest of your life.

How long would it take you to hate everything about this miracle diet?

The trick to healthy, happy, productive eating is eating with variety, intention and — most importantly — love. Love is the secret ingredient that makes all food taste good, not just your grandma's Southern cooking! When you embrace love for yourself and your body, mealtimes stop being a hassle and become a ritual of self-care and encouragement, filled with bright colors, popping spices and delicious, NutriGlam food.

Calories and macros

There are 3500 calories in a pound. So on a daily basis, how many calories do you really need? If you're a woman between 18–55, you'll need 1500–2000 calories a day to maintain weight or lose it safely [2]. Later in life, you'll need fewer calories, unless you want to look like one of those ladies who made caftans so popular as everyday clothing.

Forget everything you've heard about some weight-loss programs being better or worse than others, or some foods naturally torching fat or raising your metabolism. There's one thing that all successful diets have in common, and that's reducing calories. Cabbage soup or meal replacement bars, tiny plates, lemon water, or cider vinegar; if it curbs your appetite, you'll eat less. And when you're eating less, you're losing weight.

That doesn't mean you can eat 1500 calories of chocolate a day and still lose weight (this Glammer proved THAT through experimentation). It really does matter what you put in your mouth.

To explain this, it's helpful to understand macronutrients, or macros, and now is a great time to mention that I'm not a nutritionist and I don't play one on TV. However, ALL this stuff is pretty straightforward and can be researched online (including where to find a nutritionist). Meanwhile, I've been

studying this stuff for about thirty years, and I've done almost all of it, and the good stuff twice, so now you don't have to.

You might have heard of IIFYM (If It Fits Your Macros), a diet philosophy that states that you can eat anything you want—as long as you stay within your calorie limit, and your ratios of protein, fat and carbs.

The IIFYM approach is wildly popular for two reasons: it's simple, and it works. You'll find clinical evidence as well as testimonials online written by everyone from professional bodybuilders to ordinary moms. IIFYM is perfect for busy people and social eaters—even if you're vegan, kosher, gluten free or have allergies—because it's a supportive system, not a restrictive diet.

Online calculators and fitness professionals can help you calculate your macros. However, if you want to get started right away, there's a simple formula:

- Protein: 0.8g-1g per pound of lean bodyweight

- Fat: 0.2–0.4g per pound of lean bodyweight

- Carbs: fill up the rest of your calorie limit

Please note: 'lean bodyweight' means your total bodyweight, minus your amount of body fat. That's important—a short woman who's overweight at 180lbs will actually only need 110g-120g of protein a day, or even less. To calculate your body fat, use an online calculator or consult your doctor.

Does this mean you can eat a side of bacon for breakfast, a plate of spaghetti for lunch and mayo on your hamburger for dinner? Probably not—you won't be able to have the hamburger bun (carbs) as well as all that spaghetti... and you have to cut off the bacon fat to fit in some mayo. And that anemic piece of lettuce on your burger is NOT a salad. It's all about finding that balance between delicious, healthy, and filling.

Besides, by making sure you eat a variety of fruits and vegetables as well as good fats (olive oil, avocados, nuts) and lean protein (whether you're a meat eater or vegan), you're gifting your body plenty of vital nutrients you just don't find in Ritz crackers topped with Cheez-Whiz. Also, if you're a comfort eater, filling a huge bowl with a (non-deep-fried) vegetable you love—that your macros and calories will let you eat in near-unlimited quantities—is a great way to satisfy the crunch of mindless late-night snacking.

I also love the shift of cutting out flour and sugar completely for at least a month (I did it for over two years and it was the best I ever felt). Once you reintroduce it, the cravings are gone, and you can start to see where your patterns were and what you really want to put in your body. I still eat enough salad for four people almost every time I sit down. Making vegetables my friend has made an enormous difference in my life.

What to eat

Even rabbits can't exist on carrots alone. Whoever you are and whatever you do, you need a wholesome diet full of vegetables, lean proteins, vitamins and minerals.

Here's the formula for "what to eat":

WHOLE FOODS (which you like)
+ LOVINGLY PREPARED (by you or someone else)
+ GOOD FOR YOU (physically AND mentally)
= FOOD YOU DESERVE TO EAT (with or without your loved ones).

Whole Foods

Nope, I'm not talking about the grocery store. The term *whole foods* refers to edibles still in their purest, or most "whole" form. Think back to caveman times, when we ran around plucking berries right from the vine or dining on fresh-caught meat cooked over an open flame. There was no Crisco, no Nutella, no refrigeration — early humans got all of their nutrients straight from the source.

Today's processing systems have made it easier to grow, store, and cook food, and have also resulted in a ton of unhealthy chemicals and additives that don't agree with our systems.

Modern takeout and dine-in restaurants offer up a world of new cuisines — although many of them are steeped in butter and covered in calorie-loaded sauces. Scheduling a regular night to eat out can be a wonderful motivator to power a week of healthy eating. Thought I don't think any of us will take eating out for granted, ever again, it's important not to overdo it. You may need to adjust for extra calories if your favorite happy hour place has tempting desserts and cream-based sauces. Or, consider getting your favorite entrée and swapping out that plate of fries for a side of steamed veggies. Most chain restaurants put the calorie count on the

menu, or you can look up the recipe or calories, so you can find out if you're blowing your whole day on eleven-layer nacho dip.

You might be thinking, *I've spent my whole life eating processed foods. I love chicken nuggets, I adore Twinkies, and I HATE vegetables. How can I still eat healthy?*

I'm not going to shame you for enjoying the food you love. Here's the small print: processed food is not good for you. And we all know that. It's not mentally or physically healthy to punish yourself for the foods you eat or listen to anyone who makes you feel bad about enjoying a snack.

One more thing: if all you're doing is filling that hole in your soul, cramming your mouth so you don't have to think about the stuff that's really bothering you, please look for the deeper reasons.

Is it okay to really enjoy your food, like a love affair with an Italian, only it's an Italian menu? I can get down and get funky with an all-you-can-eat brunch or a bowl of ice cream just as much as the next Glammer. Most of us simply need more of one thing: balance.

Can't or won't give up that soda with lunch? Okay! Then swap out your sandwich for a spinach salad. You've got a long-term relationship with Pringles? Me, too! Pull a short stack out of the can, put the rest away in a sealed container (tape that sucker down if you have to!) and have some more tomorrow (or next week).

I'm going to say something radical: if you want those nachos, GO FOR IT! Just stop when you're full and choose to eat lightly for the rest of the day.

You can enjoy the foods you like (even those "bad" ones), as long as you're following serving sizes and balancing out unhealthy food choices with healthier ones.

You're here, and you're healthy enough to be exploring your options. Or, if you do have health issues, you're smart enough to know a book is no substitute for qualified medical advice from an actual doctor—right? It's all about creating a diet (remember, a diet is nothing more the things you eat) that makes you happy, inside and out.

Lovingly Prepared

I'm going to give you a gift. If you don't like to cook, *you don't have to.*

Yes, really!

One of the tricks to healthy, wholesome food is having it prepared by someone who loves to make food. If your ideal Sunday is spent grocery shopping and meal prepping for the week, well, that's me! If it makes you cringe a little, that's okay, too (and you're welcome to come to Sunday Supper at my house!)

Luckily, we're well past the age where women are automatically assumed to be fantastic cooks and excellent housekeepers, which is both awesome if that's you, and terrible if you're going to be all judgy about it every time you go to someone's house for dinner and they've made spaghetti from a jar (I'm not naming names).

If you love cooking, starting a new diet gives you the chance to explore a world full of exciting cuisines. Did you know many Indian and Asian recipes are vegan or vegetarian, or can be made so with a couple quick swaps?

And if you're not a fan of hours in the kitchen, no worries! You'll want to cut down on prep and simplify the process while keeping a focus on healthy, lightly processed foods. Nowadays, grocery stores have addressed our time crunch by offering a ton of pre-cut items (zucchini spirals, halved and cleaned Brussels sprouts, or cubed butternut squash could be in your near future!) Note: this is different from *processed* food with tons of preservatives and additives — it's one thing to buy spiralized zucchini to make zoodles at home; it's another to buy a box of fettuccine noodles and a bag of veggie potato chips and call it a day.

The trick to eating healthy as a "non-cook" is to find three or four quick, easy recipes that you *love* to eat, and *know* you can cook. From there, you can cook and freeze meals in advance,

or subscribe to a healthy eating mail service that delivers your meals to you. You don't have to eat fast food because it's the only thing ready in five minutes — you've got this.

Good For You

Prescribed diet plans, such as Jenny Craig and the South Beach Diet are very popular, and often quite successful, at least in the short term. Though for lifetime goals, they don't take into account the logistics of organizing personal eating habits, family and work schedules, or exercise preferences — at least, not to the extent where you can maintain it for the rest of your days.

Remember: the only diet that works is the one that works for YOU. There'll be some experimentation along the way, and at the end you'll have a full game plan tailored for your very own!

Veganism or being vegetarian is a great way to expand your culinary horizons and explore the discipline and open mind it takes to eat only non-animal products. Many people choose this lifestyle because they love animals, because of environmental concerns, or simply because they feel healthier and better for it; it's all good.

However, if you go vegan or strict vegetarian, please bear in mind that you may be missing out on key nutrients. Vegans

can exist solely on Oreos and French fries—that just doesn't mean they should!

Being veg has to fit in with your daily life: don't sweat over seitan or think you have to make your own Kim Chee if you don't especially like cooking. Like anyone following a new food lifestyle, it's important for you to eat lots of leafy greens, and consider bringing supplements into your daily routine. Popping a calcium tablet or multivitamin is not "cheating"—bottom line is that you want to make your own decisions.

Food You Deserve To Eat

Mindset, mindset, mindset. I said it three times because it's 3 X as important as the food you eat. Whether you made it yourself or bought it from someone who just *loves* to cook, the satisfaction we feel after a delightful, healthy, well-balanced meal is a signal of yummy sent straight to our brains. This is the food we *deserve* to eat — not empty carbs and fat that send us into a carb coma.

Let's talk treats. Hey, your dog gets cookies — why can't you? Some people can live without "a little something" every day; maybe for you, that doesn't feel optimal, or even optional. Maybe this is why food became a problem for you in the first place. It feels special, like we're rewarding ourselves; which is a beautiful thing, just not if we indulge too often in sweet or fatty treats. If I'm singing your song, see what happens when you gift yourself a little 100 calorie gift each day, such as a single-serving packet of cookies or chips, or a frozen fudge bar. One dark chocolate square, savored slowly, may be exactly what your body wants. Just not the whole thousand-calorie bar.

In my retreats, I give everyone the Conscious Chocolate Exercise, where I invite them to really use their five senses to eat a single Hershey's Kiss®. First they unwrap it, hearing the crinkle of the thin foil, smelling the first scent of unfolding chocolate, sensing their mouths begin to water. Once they pop it into their mouths, they let it melt on their tongues, waiting as long as possible before even taking the first chew. The whole process takes almost five minutes. Compare that to the last time you sucked down a whole Snickers® bar in a minute flat and called it lunch.

Try the Conscious Chocolate Exercise yourself. The idea is just to be more aware and mindful. Don't eat chocolate? Any other food will do, so long as you enjoy it in your mouth and pay attention to the process.

How to eat

Okay, so we've tackled crash diets — we've talked about *what* to eat. Now let's talk about the deep *how*.

What does it feel like to be hungry? Too many of us don't know any more. Your stomach might rumble a little, and pretty much any kind of eats sound like they would be really tasty. If you're craving a very specific food ("I want sea salt & vinegar Kettle chips, and I want them NOW!"), you might only be dehydrated. Salt cravings, specific food cravings, and dry mouth are all signs that our bodies need water. And if you're one of the vast percentage of us who don't drink enough water (guilty as charged), drinking a cool glass and waiting ten minutes can tell you if your hunger was genuine.

It's critical to *check in with your body*. If you're hungry, place your hunger level on a scale of 1-10, where 10 is the way you might feel after gorging an all-you-can-eat buffet, and a 0 means you're ready to gnaw someone's arm off if it gets too close to your face.

If you're truly hungry, you should be somewhere between a 0 and a 3. If you're at a comfortable 4 or above, give yourself twenty minutes and then check in again. When we eat meals, it's important to stop when we get to a 5 (if your goal is to lose weight) or a 6 or 7 (if your goal is to maintain the weight you're at). Many people eat to a 9 or 10 even when they aren't that hungry, and pack on extra calories they don't need. Checking in with your body to know if you're *truly* hungry — or just bored — can make a huge difference.

Another technique I love is eating a fistful of food. Did you know that naturally, your stomach is approximately the same size as your closed fist? The stomach is super stretchy, though, so it's easy to eat much more than you need simply because there's still room. If all you ever ate was an amount the size of your closed fist, and only when you were actually hungry, you'd lose all the weight you wanted. See, I told you that simple and easy aren't the same thing!

Many people wonder if they should eat breakfast. If you feel guilt for skipping "the most important meal of the day," don't!

If breakfast is a habit your body just refuses to adopt, no matter how many times you try to wake up with a bowl of granola, it may be a sign that's just how your body functions best. Forcing the issue won't help. My whole life I loved breakfast. Now I rarely eat before noon. So I've switched to what I call "brunch salad" — loads of raw veggies topped with a hard-boiled egg, half an avocado, and a crumbled slice of uncured bacon. TA-DA! A balanced solution for both my nutritional needs and my personal desires.

Fasting, which used to be associated with religious practices or political protests, has become a more mainstream behavior in recent years as people have rediscovered its health benefits.

Intermittent fasting (IF) is another dietary system that's gained attention. Athletes and we ordinary folk alike swear by it. It's simply the process of fasting *a little,* regularly, in any pattern you like. A complete fast one day, or for sixteen hours of the day, for example.

Sound scary? It really isn't — once you consider that we're asleep for eight to nine hours of the day, and that many of us aren't hungry for a few hours before bed, it becomes a lot easier to imagine. Many people find that they sleep better and are more energized after giving their digestive systems a real break.

If you're not a fan of just drinking water, then anything under 50 calories won't trigger your digestive system too much. That

means that tea and coffee are perfectly fine during a fast. A simple 16-hour fast would involve eating your last meal around 7:00 PM, having a cup of chamomile tea before bed, and not eating your next meal until around 11:00 the next morning. After a few days, it becomes routine to skip breakfast while you go through your morning, then look forward to a meal around lunchtime. You may even be doing this naturally, without realizing! I usually eat between noon and 8PM, because that's what makes my body happy. On nights when I go back for an additional serving after that, it's harder for me to unwind for sleep.

Others swear by "the 5:2 diet," where you eat normally five days of the week, and fast for two days. Followers of this diet plan eat according to their usual diet during their five days, then consume less than 500 calories on "fast" days.

The simplicity of the diet and the fact you can eat pretty much what you like five days a week are key to its popularity. There are no restrictions on the types of food you can eat, and it is suggested that women can expect to lose about a pound a week on the diet. The jury is still out on whether intermittent fasting is healthier for you, or whether it's the simple reduction in calories which contributes to weight loss [3].

My cousins (a married couple) have stayed super lean well into their 50s by eating a really restrictive diet 6 days a week

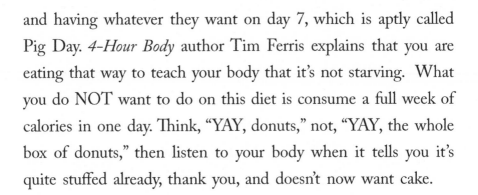

and having whatever they want on day 7, which is aptly called Pig Day. *4-Hour Body* author Tim Ferris explains that you are eating that way to teach your body that it's not starving. What you do NOT want to do on this diet is consume a full week of calories in one day. Think, "YAY, donuts," not, "YAY, the whole box of donuts," then listen to your body when it tells you it's quite stuffed already, thank you, and doesn't now want cake.

How to resist food pushers

Sigh... even though they mean well, food pushers can make it even more difficult for you to stick with your program, any program.

You know the type: grandmas, friends, and moms who love to see you eat and are always heaping seconds, thirds, and fourths onto your plate.

For someone becoming more true to themselves and discovering what they really want out of life, it doesn't help to be hounded at the dinner table by someone who says, "Go on, it's only one bite!" when you're already full... or the food's not in your chosen diet... or you don't even like what's being served!

Most food pushers are well-intentioned people who equate eating with love: either they're "feeders," who derive their

self-worth from caring for others, or they get such joy out of food themselves that they want you to have more of it (yes, I've been guilty of both these practices in the past). Both are perfectly innocent; the problem is that our Western diet is notoriously bad, and any kind of emotional attachment to mealtime is likely to result in overeating and unhealthiness.

Even worse: some Beautycons get their thrills by sabotaging your healthy efforts. They can be overweight themselves and terrified of you "leaving" them if you get healthier. They may resent you for wanting to better yourself, or they enjoy being the "skinny" one. No matter the case, these food pushers can be toxic to your well-being.

So how do you deal with this kind of well-meaning pressure? With diplomacy and grace, you NutriGlammer!

The pusher might say, "It's my specialty," or, "I baked it just for you."

Offer: "That's so sweet! I'll save it for later." Stalling is a useful tactic in these cases because you've already accepted what they see as their gift.

Be honest: "Mom, I love how much you love me, and that you show that love through the beautiful cookies you just baked. I'd love to take them home and share them with my

office." She'll hear that you know she loves you, which is where she was coming from anyway.

Then there are the passive-aggressive pushers, who say things like, "Don't be a buzzkill," or "You need some meat on those bones."

If the feeder starts commenting on your body or your choice to pursue a different way of eating, use humor to deflect the situation: "I'm in training for the Miss America contest."

Or simply tell the truth: "I've given up flour for now. No exceptions, and I feel so much better this way!"

You don't owe these feeders anything — especially not your health and self-esteem.

Over time, your mindset of allowing your own body to come first over your fear of hurting someone else's feelings may even show a pusher a thing or two about their own nutrition or behavior. Stick to your guns!

Growing your own food

Though it might seem intimidating at first, if you want to grow and gather your own organic produce at home, it's simple. Given the recent changes in the world, relying on

your own food sources could be a great choice you hadn't previously considered.

First, get your dreams in perspective: unless you already live there, you probably aren't moving to a small ranch in the rural countryside just to start a garden. Even if you can't pull whole carrots out of the earth, or spare four square feet for a vegetable patch, or even have a yard, you can add delicious home-grown greens to your diet.

All you need is a sunny windowsill, some compost, and some patience; the rest is easy to find, or you might already have it around the house.

Containers, for example—takeout containers, the clear tub kind, make great propagators. Fill halfway up with moist soil, press in your seeds, then put the lid on for cover. As soon as the green shoots start to grow, take the lid off so they have room—and when the third leaf appears, that's when you have to transfer them to their own pots.

As for seeds, you can find them in your local gardening store, some hardware stores or even supermarkets. Or, harvest them from fresh produce such as lemons, bell peppers, apples, and tomatoes. If you live in a warmer climate, you can even grow peaches, oranges, or avocados (start avos from a small tree, since they take 7 years to give fruit!)

It's easy to think growing is a lot more hassle than it is, especially when gardening websites are full of information about soil PH, lighting and hardy zones. Honestly, all you need to start is a little soil, some light, and the drive to experiment.

Have you ever ordered a steak in a fancy restaurant, and seen a bunch of tiny greens artfully placed atop your filet? Or ordered a "superfood salad," and been struck

by the colorful little sprouts that replaced your normal lettuce? These are *microveg*—and the gourmet industry is crazy about them. Microveg typically sells for $15-$25 a pound, even crazier when you realize that this cute, nutritional powerhouse is actually only tiny seeds, grown for a short length of time [4].

Some of the most popular microveg are actually pea shoots, broccoli, and beet seeds: common vegetables, harvested in seedling form. In other words, marketing genius, since they are great for you and totally cheap to grow!

Microveg is perfect to grow at home on your windowsill, and they add an instant dose of oomph to any omelet, sandwich, or salad. Best of all, most only take days to reach that perfect balance of crunch and sweetness—just don't leave them too long, because then you might as well wait until the actual vegetable arrives!

If you start small, you may find yourself really getting into gardening. These days, there's a gardening trend for everyone. Got just a small space for planting? Try a vertical garden system that's a self-contained kit (I love the JuicePlus Tower Garden and I have one myself). Want to stop wasting resources? Rip up water-sucking grass in favor of growing veggies as your own front yard – raised boxes can supply enough for your family and likely the neighbors, too.

In your back yard, consider simply mixing vegetable plants into flowerbeds for seasonal color that keeps on giving.

Starting in World War I, people were asked to plant Victory Gardens. Between 1917 and 1918, over 5.2 million gardens were planted and raised, creating an estimated 1.45 million quarts of canned fruits and vegetables. This practice was continued again in World War II, and the Victory Gardens saved many from food chain supply issues as rations took effect. [5]

In today's uncertain world, we have all recently seen how fragile our own supply chains can be. Creating your own garden, especially during times when we may need to stay home for extended periods of time, may turn out to be more essential than just a hobby. Many gardeners find planting, growing, even weeding, to be soothing or meditative, and it certainly ensures you interact with nature. If you haven't gardened before, now may be the perfect time to consider it.

Eat a good diet, take care of your skin — Your spirit will shine both outside and within!

What you eat shows up in the way you look every day. I know for me, as I've gotten older, I really have to ask if I want that

second glass of wine, knowing that when I wake up tomorrow, my eyes may suddenly look like I've packed actual luggage under them. Bread or pizza is an invitation for my pants to be tight the next morning. Everything you put in your mouth is a choice to be weighed, no pun intended. It will affect your body, especially your body's largest organ — your skin.

In addition to eating more than the recommended quantities of fruits and vegetables ("Salad for four? Nope — that's just my lunch!"), I often supplement with powerful nutrients such as collagen, vitamin C, and fatty fish oils. Though I'd love to get all my nutrition from food, the truth is that as we hit that later period in life, we all need a little help staying ageless. The important thing is that you make the right choice for you. When selecting supplements, look for brands you trust, results from real customer reviews, and ingredients that are clear (if you don't recognize it, look it up — the internet, as always, is your friend).

If your skin needs more help, focus on eating what's best for it, like salmon from sustainably farmed resources, organic strawberries and blueberries, kale and spinach, and cutting back on alcohol, flour and sugar. Then be sure to treat your skin daily with the right routine for your skin type.

NutriGlamorous has a great line of helpful products on Amazon, because it can be hard to find a good resource that

you can trust. We prefer products that are as close to nature as possible and that will give great results, and you should, too — whatever products you choose to use. What's most expensive isn't necessarily the best!

"For me, exercise is more than just physical—it's therapeutic."

— Michelle Obama

Move

I f you hate exercise, Glammer, you're not alone.

Many of us dream of having a trim waist, slim thighs or toned arms like the former First Lady—it just doesn't feel easy fitting in an exercise regime along with all our other commitments. Especially if we don't enjoy it that much.

Exercise improves outward beauty, yes… and it's a free anti-depressant, which helps refresh and replenish our minds as well as our bodies. After all, the brain is an organ, too. With so much stress weighing on our minds these days, it's more important than ever to make sure our brains are physically fit to withstand and alleviate the pressure.

In fact, it's an essential part of life. If we expand our understanding of exercise beyond skintight yoga pants and chocolate-flavored protein powder, we can acknowledge that moving our bodies simply enables us to explore and interact with the world. In fact, your world can become your new gym, which can be very important on a shelter-in-place or post-pandemic planet.

Connect with your YES

Human beings respond to two things: pleasure and pain. We move toward pleasure and away from pain. In his book

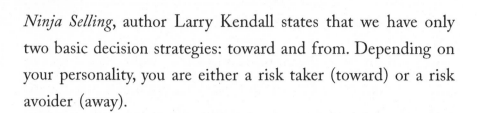
Ninja Selling, author Larry Kendall states that we have only two basic decision strategies: toward and from. Depending on your personality, you are either a risk taker (toward) or a risk avoider (away).

The trouble with exercise for most of us is that it can cause mental pain (*I'm not where I want to be, my body isn't doing well here, I suck*) or physical pain (*I'm sore, this hurts, why do I feel like someone just stabbed me in the knee?*) So the very thing we would like, the pleasure of having a healthy body or fitting into that dress, is at the end of a road that may be paved with a bunch of pain potholes.

You want to change your relationship to exercise? First change your thoughts about what it is. Because if you're thinking that it's a struggle, and you are lousy at it, you are likely going to move away from the pain of it or towards the pleasure of something else.

Why are you exercising anyway? What's the result you want, and what would you like your pleasurable journey to the island of fabulous to look like? For me, a key for beginning to enjoy exercise was to treat the whole experience as a delight. Choosing yoga and listening to inspirational speakers, instead of going to a sweaty crowded gym, made a huge difference. Slowing down and being really present to the magnificent machine of my body, being grateful as I began accomplishing

full pushups, or extending the length of time I could plank —
those changes really helped. I always reward myself with
a few breaths at the end of a session, to connect with my
body and feel how truly happy it is, now that the aches and
pains I woke up with are gone.

Create pleasure during your exercise time, small victories you
can move towards, and eliminate focusing on the pain of
your experience. It's always NutriGlam to focus on what you

want, and to ignore what you don't want. So ask yourself, where is your YES? Connect with that and allow it to change everything, breath by breath.

How to move more

You've read or heard the basics: 'take the stairs instead of the elevator' or 'get off the bus two stops early,' and those things help, when they are part of a bigger shift. Of course, trying to adopt habits you don't even like in the first place is the fast-track route to becoming a Beautycon—dimming your own light to please someone else's idea of a perfect you.

We want to enjoy exercise, get results, and move more. How do we do it? By welcoming any form of movement that brings joy into our lives, making the time and space for it, and exploring possibilities outside of fashion trends.

PS. Yes, it's awesome to look great in your hot pink yoga pants if you want them. Just don't feel obligated to buy the 6-month package to Pure Barre when you hate the way the perky instructor tells you to "move into your split stretch," when you can only get your legs far enough apart to straddle a bike.

Take a few moments to think how different ways moving more could improve your work life. Instead of eating a sack

lunch at your desk, could you take the whole hour and walk to the cafe on the next block? It might cost a little more, and you wouldn't be answering emails over lunch; instead, you would come back more refreshed every day. Whether you work from home or in an office setting, getting away from your desk to recharge your batteries is key to being more productive throughout the rest of your day. Or, if your lunch break is seven steps from the kitchen, could you set a timer to refill your water bottle hourly?

Consider a standing desk at work, which can also help you to release weight and stay active. Take a five-minute "turn about the room" every hour (apparently, characters in Jane Austen novels understood this basic stroll to break up all the sitting they were doing). Look online for exercises you can do at your desk if you have no way of getting up.

Maybe you're in a physically demanding job, such as postal worker or outdoor supervisor, beset by aches and pains, and with only the energy to order takeout when you collapse onto the couch after a long day. You don't want to move more—you have to move better!

Whatever your level of activity, stretch often, as much as possible. Explore yoga, Tai Chi, or other mindful ways to move the body, and incorporate these as much as you can in your daily routine. You've seen dogs or cats get up — they stretch, every time, and there's a reason. If you can, consult a professional physiotherapist, or redirect those weekly takeout expenses for a massage on the weekends. There are home-based services that cost a lot less than a spa, if you're on a budget, or both hand-held and seated massagers if you prefer to purchase one for your home.

Resolve to eat healthier (see the *Eat* chapter), because carrying less weight reduces stress on your knees and back. And remember: never, ever punish yourself. Reward your body for the hard work it does by fueling it properly and letting it relax.

How to find your favorite exercise

Looking for enjoyable exercise? Here's a hint: it's probably not on a DVD in the Fitness section at Walmart!

It's in your childhood, biking up the road or hiking with your parents. Riding horses, swimming in lakes, or playing ball with your brother. It may have been that one fencing class you took at college years ago, and still think about.

Here's the thing: when you move your body, your mind is often bored.

Oh, her outfit is cute!

This position is so stupid!

I'm thirsty.

When will this be OVER?

The best exercise keeps your mind engaged, because it helps pass the time and we don't even realize you're "eating your vegetables" and doing something good for yourself. So, though exercises like yoga and dance (which invite you to think on the spot) are good, exercises you're truly passionate about, and love studying while you improve your technique, are even better.

Can you try new classes, or revisit old sports you loved as a kid? If they're available, check your local sports centers and libraries for information about adult leagues, or even consider starting one yourself. Give yourself the gift of exploration and see which ones you love. My favorite is salsa dance, and I take lessons on YouTube!

Remember: the only exercise plan that works is the one that works for you. That's why you need to track three essential factors to know if your workout is working [6]:

1. Happiness. You enjoy what you are doing, you look forward to your exercise, and you find that you can "lose yourself" while doing it — it's a form of relaxation.

This will be your first benefit if you're starting from scratch (with a new attitude to match!)

2. Health. You can do the things you want to do without feeling slow, lethargic or unwell, and you've got a clean bill of health from your doctor. If you're not there yet, work towards it with more exercise. Instead of giving up and saying that you can't do it, even simple stretches can build towards better health.

3. Looks. You feel great about how you look (or at least, better than you did) and you're comfortable in your own skin. You're confident walking down the street, and your outsides match your inside personality. If you're not there yet, keep up the action and you will start to see a difference in just a few weeks.

There are an almost infinite number of ways to boost these three factors, and every Glammer reading this book will have her own version of what works.

That means there's no wrong form of exercise!

If you're a mom who last worked out in college, your happy relaxation exercise will be a lot different than a volleyball player's. If you're an aspiring bodybuilder, your ideal 'look good naked' body will be very different from a woman who just wants to lose her muffin top.

If you're an athlete, your idea of healthy might be running a marathon or a 6-minute mile, and without them, you wouldn't consider yourself healthy, whereas you might be happy to simply lower your cholesterol, or not get winded playing with your kids.

A gentle reminder: if you love endurance sports such as running or cycling, you cannot expect to get a sculpted physique as well, unless you're always bodybuilding. Certain activities will shape your body a different way, so consider the kind of body you'd like to have and tailor your exercise to it. It's perfectly okay to just want to be healthier and not even care what type of body you shift into.

The importance of walking

A good walk can cure many things, from restlessness to an irritable mood or sadness, to the urge to explore or reconnect with nature. During a shelter-in-place period, many of us have seen first-hand, how stuck we feel without the ability to move outside.

Walking upright on two legs is more fundamentally important than we realize; thousands of years ago, our ancestors stood on two feet to spot predators. It meant babies were more vulnerable, as they had to be born earlier to fit through our

narrower, upright-walking pelvis, and so had to stay with their mamas longer. Put simply, it was because we could walk that we developed nuclear families [7].

So, what better way to connect with who we are deep inside, to our sense of community and our belonging here on planet Earth?

Today there are no predators waiting to eat us, so we can walk however and whenever we please. If where you live is surrounded by highways, even a walk around the block makes a welcome change of scene. Or, you can travel to walk somewhere special. It might seem strange to take a trip just to walk, yet once you've done it you may very well get addicted to a lovely outdoor spot, or several!

If the thought of simply wandering around doesn't grab you, consider fitting in some extra steps in your everyday life. Can you get up earlier and catch another bus, getting off a few stops early and walking to work through the park? Even ten minutes of walking a day will make a difference to your heart health, your weight, and your mood [8].

The average person walks about 2–3 miles an hour, depending on age, weight, and if you're carrying things or stopping to take photos. That burns roughly 160–180 calories an hour; if that doesn't sound like a lot, remember that walking tones your muscles and improves cardiovascular health as well [9]. As an added benefit (unlike running or the stair machine) walking is so natural it gets easier much more quickly, leading you to take longer or brisker walks without even noticing. It's low-impact on the knees, and social—especially if you walk to a friend's house or you're in a neighborhood where everyone is walking their dogs.

Being NutriGlamorous is all about knowing and taking care of your authentic self, inside and out—and walking is the perfect way to get to know who that is. Carving out time in your schedule to physically move from point to point reminds you of the progress you've made. You can use it as moving meditation: let your breath normalize into the rhythm of your steps, put some calming music on headphones, or simply listen to the sounds of the city or nature surrounding you and let your thoughts wander. Or listen to a podcast or audiobook for some entertainment or self-improvement.

Walking can be a wonderful escape, even if we have no destination in mind.

How to keep fit in front of the TV

OK, so... what if you don't like sports, or you live in a really cold climate —or you're in a long-term relationship with your TV?

79

Congrats, you can still be NutriGlamorous! Some of us would rather catch up on our favorite shows than break a sweat. And that's okay. It's about finding your own path—and despite what a lot of Beautycons tell you, it's perfectly possible to honor your body with exercise while indulging in TV or your favorite movies. Wouldn't you rather watch something you enjoy instead of another fitness celebrity workout? (Well, there *was* that one with Chris Hemsworth working out during the pandemic...)

Remember I told you earlier that the best exercises keep your mind engaged? Yes, the latest episode of your favorite show counts! Many exercise gurus advocate quick bursts of exercise during commercial breaks; there's no reason you shouldn't exercise throughout the entire show if you want. When you watch TV, your body is just lying there on the couch doing nothing—so you might as well make it move! The main thing to remember is, of course, your mind will be busy digesting the latest plot twists... so it's best to choose a simple exercise. Sit ups are great, and so is running on the spot, or using a treadmill or a bike if you have one. (Yes, my elliptical is in the family room — which is the only place I remember to use it!) I also do yoga in front of the TV, though advanced poses might be a little counterproductive if you can't see the screen through your backwards triangle pose.

I also love my core roller, which uses my body weight to roll across my muscles. It also helps to massage your fascia, the important and often-neglected connective tissue that (in my non-medical brain) basically holds your body together under your skin. If you haven't used one, just get it. For me, it feels wonderful and helps me to stretch and relieves pain. More flexibility is always a good thing.

Here's a great list of 25 no-equipment exercises for you to check out. If you group them together in sets of five, and do

a variety of reps (aim for 3 sets of each, 12-15 reps per set) during your favorite show, you can watch nearly half a season before you have to start over! Or just listen to some calm or vibrant music — it's up to you!

This is a good time to mention that I'm a mindset coach, not a fitness trainer. So let's use some logic: Go slow and build up to a regular program if you haven't done this in a long time. Add on every week until you're doing the suggestions in the above paragraph easily. If it hurts when you do it, is it a good hurt (I haven't done this in a long time) or a bad hurt (it's making my hips ache)? Are you out of shape or overweight enough to need to see a doctor first, before even getting off the couch? Do it. This isn't about blaming yourself for what you haven't done, it's about moving into a NutriGlamorous attitude, so you can start shifting your body from the inside!

If these instructions seem too complicated, look up how-to videos online.

1. Inchworm

Stand up tall, legs straight, and bend down so your fingertips graze the floor. Keeping your legs straight (not locked), slowly lower your body to the floor, and then walk your hands forward. Once you get to a push-up position, start taking tiny steps so your feet meet your hands.

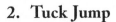

2. Tuck Jump

Standing with your knees slightly bent, jump up as high as you can and bring your knees in towards your chest while extending your arms straight in front of you. Land with your knees slightly bent and quickly jump again.

3. Bear Crawl

Get on all fours, rise up on your toes, tighten your core, and slowly reach forward with your right arm and right knee, then your left arm and left knee, as you crawl across the floor.

4. Mountain Climber

These are powerful! Starting in plank position with your feet about shoulder-width apart, bring your left foot forward directly under your chest while keeping your right leg straight. Keep your hands on the ground and keep your core muscles tight, then walk or jump to switch legs. Your left leg should now be extended behind your body with your right knee forward. Alternate legs, getting faster if you are comfortable with it, until you are moving quickly. Bonus points if you imagine yourself scaling a mountain.

5. Standard Push-Up

This one is a classic, because it works. Place your hands on the floor, shoulder-width apart, keep the feet flexed and hip distance apart, and tighten your core. Bend your elbows —

keeping them close at your side — until your chest reaches the ground, then push back up. See how many you can do in an ad break!

6. March on the Spot with Bicep Curl

Grab some heavy household objects, like full half-gallon plastic bottles or quart cans (or hand weights if you've got them) and briskly march on the spot while alternating arms, bending at the elbow to bring your hand up to your shoulder.

7. All Fours Walkout

Begin on all your hands and knees with your belly core engaged, then slowly walk your hands forward, staying on your toes and keeping your feet stationary. Slowly walk your hands backwards to the starting position, maintaining stability and balance. Surprisingly effective!

8. Burpees

This classic exercise is one of the most effective bodyweight exercises ever. Start out in a low squat position with hands on the floor. Next, kick the feet back to a push-up position, complete one push-up, then immediately return the feet to the squat position. Leap up as high as possible before squatting and moving back into the push-up position. (Oversharing tip: If I eat even 2 hours before I do these, they make me burp!)

9. Plank

Simply lie looking down at the floor with your forearms on the floor and your hands clasped. Extend your legs behind your body and rise up on your toes. Keeping your back straight, tighten your abs and hold for as long as you can. You can also do this on fully extended arms, or alternate lifting one leg at a time for 15 or 30 seconds. Planking is a tough one to start — and will work wonders for your whole core. It's my favorite.

10. Plank-to-Push-Up

Starting in the plank position you used above, place down one hand at a time to lift up into a push-up position, with your back straight and your core engaged. Then move one arm at a time back into plank. When you repeat, alternate arms.

11. Wall Sit

Stand with your back against the wall and slowly slide down until your thighs are parallel to the ground – you will be sitting against the wall with your legs at a 90º angle. Make sure your knees are directly above your ankles and keep your back straight. Do this one for 30 seconds at least. My other favorite!

12. Lunge

Stand with your hands on your hips and your feet hip-width apart. Step your right leg forward and slowly lower your body until your left knee is near to the floor and bent at least 90

degrees. Return to the starting position and repeat on the other side. Remember to always keep your knee directly in line with your foot!

13. Clock Lunge

Switch up your lunges by doing one, then taking a big step to the right and lunging in that direction. Lunge on your left leg, taking another big step to the right, and go all the way around the clock face. Good for commercials since you can't see the TV part of the time!

14. Lunge-to-Row

Do a normal lunge, then pull your arms into a rowing position by bending at the elbow and keeping your arms tucked close. Keep your leg bent at about 90 degrees, then return to the starting position. Repeat on the other side.

15. Pistol Squat

Standing holding your arms straight out in front, raise your right leg, flexing your right ankle and pushing your hips back. Then lower your body while keeping your right leg raised. Hold as long as you can, then return to standing.

16. Lunge Jump

Lunge forward with your right foot. Jump straight up, propelling your arms forward while keeping your elbows bent. While in

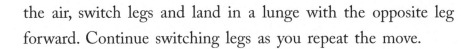

the air, switch legs and land in a lunge with the opposite leg forward. Continue switching legs as you repeat the move.

17. Curtsy Lunge

When lunging, step your left leg back behind the right, bending your knees and lowering your hips until your right thigh is almost parallel to the floor. Keep your back straight and hips facing forward, and go slowly so you can correct your positioning if it's twisting your knees.

18. Squat

The classic! Stand with your feet parallel or turned out 15 degrees, whatever's comfortable. Slowly crouch by bending your hips and knees until your thighs are at least parallel to the floor. Make sure your heels do not rise off the floor. Slowly rise, keeping your heels down, until you're standing up.

19. Single Leg Deadlift

Stand with your feet together, then lift your right leg a little and lower your arms and torso while raising your right leg behind the body. Keep your left knee slightly bent and reach the arms as close to the floor as possible. Raise the torso while lowering the right leg, then switch legs.

20. Squat Reach and Jump

Do a normal squat, and then jump up, reaching your arms high overhead. This is surprisingly tough, so hang in there!

21. Chair Squat

Stand with your feet hip-distance apart and squat until your thighs are parallel to the floor while swinging your arms up. Straighten your legs, then lift your right knee while swinging your left arm outside your right knee. Return to standing and repeat on the other side.

22. Quadruped Leg Lift

Starting on your hands and knees, keep your back flat and engage your core. Raise your left leg straight back, stopping when your foot is hip level and your thigh parallel to the floor. Balance for as long as possible, then raise your bottom right toe off the floor, tightening your butt, back, and abs (try to be graceful here!) Hold for up to 10 seconds, then switch legs.

23. Step-Up

Use a footstool or sturdy box (or the bottom step of a staircase), then step your right foot on top. Step up until your right leg is straight, and your left foot is still not touching down. Lower yourself down, then repeat, switching sides after as many reps as you can handle.

24. Calf Raise

This one you can do anywhere — simply come up on your tip-toes. Keep your knees straight and heels off the floor, hold

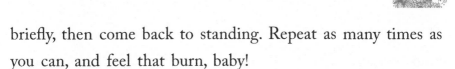

briefly, then come back to standing. Repeat as many times as you can, and feel that burn, baby!

25. Russian Twist

Lie on your back with your knees bent and your feet flat on your mat or carpet. Place your hands at your waist, making fists (your elbows will be bent). Come up halfway, as if you were starting a situp, then twist to one side and touch your fists to the mat. Twist to the other side and touch the mat. Do as many as you can for one commercial, or thirty seconds, or until your sides begin to ache in a good way.

The importance of moving for joy, instead of shame

So many of us get trapped in an endless cycle of depriving our body of joyful movement, shaming ourselves for it, then punishing ourselves even further by engaging in exercise we don't like.

Isn't it time for us to break that cycle?

First, make a definite decision that you are going to create something just for you. No guilt, no shame, no punishment.

Humans love movement naturally—it's time to find the kind of exercise that will truly move you. Instead of buying countless more products, powders, pills and programs that don't work because they don't "spark joy"—recognize life is too short not to dance, challenge yourself, and follow your desire for a healthy body.

On the whole, exercise is a pretty level playing field. As long as you end up breathing heavily, sweating a little, and maybe feel a little sore in the morning, you can be sure your workout is doing its job. So, the question is not if it will work—almost any exercise will shed extra pounds, improve your flexibility or tone your muscles.

The real question is: are you willing to give it a chance?

In other words, will you want to do the exercise often enough for it to have an effect?

Once you realize you may have been bullying, cajoling and pleading with yourself to do something you were never meant to do (for weeks if not months or years), it's time to forgive yourself: and start scheduling some serious "Personal Me Time."

The first time I heard that phrase was from a makeup artist on a movie set I was working on. I was the Executive Producer, which sounds NutriGlam, right? Think 18-hour days and

crushing responsibility instead. She grabbed me one day, sat me down in her chair, said, "You need some 'Personal Me Time,'" and proceeded to give me a makeover. I felt so pampered and cared for. Everyone needs a dose of Personal Me Time, as far as I'm concerned.

One great way of making sure you get enough of the right kind of exercise is to pencil it in. Make it a daily, weekly,

and monthly commitment to get up and move in one of your favorite ways. This is different from how you'll schedule a work call or your kid's soccer practice—let it feel like you're taking the last cookie, stealing the best moments from your calendar and planting the self-care flag firmly in those spots. This already sounds more fun, doesn't it? Remember this is how to choose to move towards what you want and desire, and away from what you don't want.

It doesn't matter if you're taking a Pilates class, running with a buddy, doing some mindful yoga in a quiet corner of the park or practicing sit-ups while rewatching the entire first season of Gilmore Girls—this time is sacred! Don't let a Beautycon, or anyone else, tell you that your preferred exercise isn't good enough. After all, it's getting you off your butt and that makes it great!

Refuse other commitments. Move stuff around! Make it feel like an indulgence — a daily spa visit for your mind and your muscles (which it is).

Being a Glammer is all about learning how to prioritize important things that have been neglected over the years, to sink into your true self like a warm bath… indulgent, healthy, and delicious. We deserve it!

And… you need to give yourself time and space to decouple from the Beautycon exercise industry: all the fake

transformations, the glossy profile pictures and high pressure to give 110% every single day. Even Beautycons who are preaching balance, who are taking regular rest days and posting pictures of their bloated tummies with laugh-crying emojis, are an unhealthy influence on you if you feel sad, unworthy or not good enough when you look at them.

Be a Glammer who says NO to anything that doesn't lift you up spiritually, emotionally, or physically.

That said, it's important to recognize many of us will have tangled feelings of guilt around exercise, and if you're snapping at friends or family or avoiding things you used to love even social media because you feel ashamed, please do whatever it takes to forgive yourself — it's time to accept that part of your life. Open your mind, and admit to yourself where you may not have lived up to your expectations. It's okay—because you're going to make a new choice, this time for good. You can do it.

"When I fall in love, it will be forever."

— *Jane Austen*

Love 4

Love is one of the most powerful forces on the planet, no wonder none of us gets it right a hundred percent of the time.

It's also a major factor in many areas of our lives beyond our romantic partners — our families, our social lives, even our smartphone habits are all tied up in the tricky tentacles of love, with all its joys and sorrows.

Love is the fuel that will either carry you on your journey to becoming a true Glammer, or leave you a flaming wreck— and if you've had a bad breakup, toxic friendship or simply struggle to love yourself, you're all too familiar with love's undesirable side effects.

My mission is to help you fall back in love with love. I promise not to get too treacly, and in turn, please promise yourself that you will keep an open mind, especially if you've given up on love.

Do you love yourself?

Self-love is vital to every life. Without it, you will always feel like you don't really deserve your happiness; like someone might show up and take it all away from you. Or worse, you'll never really be happy.

If you love yourself, awesome!! If not, it's time to look in a mirror. No really, I mean bring this book over to your closest mirror and take a good look. See you in there? You're awesome! You know how I know? You're here, aren't you? There's no entrance exam to self-love, no continuing education fees, no gatekeeper or Mother Superior or parent or government official to tell you what's acceptable and what's not. You were born deserving it, and nothing you have done in your life, no matter what anyone says, can change that. There are no accidents in God (and nope – you're not the first!) So you might as well start loving yourself!

Here's how:

Look in the mirror and say, "I love myself." Go on (no one is looking, and no one will know!) Now say it again. Slowly is fine. Just get the words out once. Then again. Then smile and go on with your day. Tonight, do it again. In fact, do it every day for a week. By then, it will be much easier. You know why? Because your "I Love Myself" face is all rusty, just like the Tin Man in *The Wizard of Oz*. He had rusted completely because he hadn't moved in so long. Your I Love Myself face will get oiled and start working better, too – just as soon as you start to use it.

The first time I created this exercise was about 30 years ago, because I was just so shocked that my friend didn't love

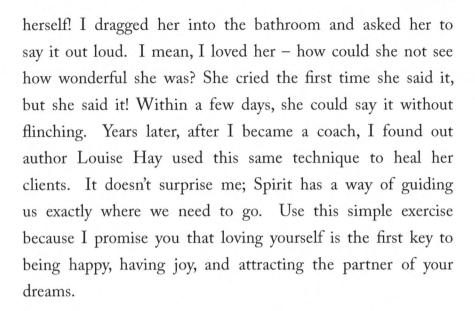

herself! I dragged her into the bathroom and asked her to say it out loud. I mean, I loved her – how could she not see how wonderful she was? She cried the first time she said it, but she said it! Within a few days, she could say it without flinching. Years later, after I became a coach, I found out author Louise Hay used this same technique to heal her clients. It doesn't surprise me; Spirit has a way of guiding us exactly where we need to go. Use this simple exercise because I promise you that loving yourself is the first key to being happy, having joy, and attracting the partner of your dreams.

Making time for your partner

The next (and most obvious) person you think about when you hear the word 'love' is your significant other—the one you have, the one you were meant to have, or the one who hasn't found you yet.

Hectic schedules and daily pressures make it more difficult than ever to even schedule a night of romance, never mind a whirlwind Austen-esque attachment. Yet quality time is vital to a healthy relationship.

Embarking on a meaningful relationship is a lot like learning to love yourself — you need to open your heart and allow

in both love and joy, which is all truly NutriGlamorous. Whether that other half resides in someone else, or simply in a neglected corner of your own self, love is about bringing those two halves together. It takes time and hard work, and it reaps wonderful rewards.

In case you don't remember, *Bridget Jones' Diary* is a modern-day retelling of *Sense & Sensibility*. In it, author Helen Fielding cleverly coins the phrase Singleton to describe women who are

currently (or perpetually) not in a relationship with said significant other. Since this may even be a life choice — the modern woman is not necessarily completed by a man — remember that you can be a Singleton and love every part of yourself.

Ideally, you'll find quiet time for yourself and your significant other (this is a great mindfulness practice if you're single, too!) It could be taking a walk, a full-blown three-course meal, or simply folding the laundry. A purpose to work towards, and a shared goal, is ideal: so instead of driving to pick your kid up from hockey, suggest you both walk there instead. Or take a bath with you and your love, enjoy a quiet conversation in a new restaurant, a joint DIY project or grocery shopping together. Just make sure whatever you choose doesn't trigger bad feelings. If one of you hates Italian waiters, getting mayonnaise, or putting up shelves, it's best to pick something else to do together.

Watching TV together is not a great idea for bonding, mainly because it's mundane while seeming to occupy you, and doesn't require your imagination. By all means, Netflix and chillax, then for quality time, unplug the screens—you'll want to create a space for you both to be yourselves, talk, and listen. Feeling stuck at home? Recreate a trip you took, or plan a new one you would love to go on.

Singletons, this all goes for you, too: go to the movies, or out to dinner. Walk by yourself, and give your inner monologue

the voice of a good friend. Date yourself and you may find your perfect partner around the corner.

How to argue well

Let's face it — even in the best relationships, there are bound to be some disagreements. It's always a good thing to have your ideas challenged and engage in some healthy debate. It's just when that debate happens with your partner or spouse, things can get a little heated (or downright ugly).

Very few of us ever learned how to argue well. We need to keep a healthy relationship top priority, sometimes even before our own personal interests. We also get to practice the art of sincere listening and effectively communicating uncomfortable truths around our honest feelings and emotions. Arguing can bring out the worst in both of you, yet there are ways you can prepare to limit the damage.

First, it's important to remember that you have each other's best interests at heart. Though your loved one might not agree with you right now, they're not being malicious, petty or engaging in pointless fights — unless there are underlying issues you both need to address.

When you argue about the things you cooperate on, such as doing the laundry or taking the kids to music lessons, treating

your partner as your bitter enemy will defeat your objective before you've even begun. The goal is to be a team; stop drawing lines in the sand and look for ways you can both compromise. Is your language coming from a place of attack or cooperation? Sometimes simply asking questions about what they think and how they would approach the problem works wonders for opening up lines of fair and even-handed communication. As my cousin pointed out when she saw how I was treating my new husband many long years ago, "Would you rather be right, or alone?"

Next is timing: do your best to refrain from bringing up contentious issues with your partner unless you can both hash it out with plenty of time to spare. A ticking clock heightens anxiety, and may lead to hasty decisions and important things going unsaid.

Bringing up a problem five minutes before you leave for work, for example, is just asking for trouble. Instead, put it aside for later, when you're both relaxed and can be responsive. Often delaying those hard conversations can help to defuse feelings, which can mean using cooperative words instead of cutting ones.

Of course, sometimes this is not easy. You are making a choice, committing to the relationship more than to the argument, and setting your feelings aside — refusing to let the issue seethe and cloud your entire day, and realizing that

even though it isn't brought up in the heat of the moment, it's still important enough for discussion.

Since we are all living busy lives, this could mean you need to plan ahead. Scheduling difficult conversations may sound like the worst idea in the world. Who wants their relationship relegated to a calendar appointment, right? And not even for a date! When you think about it, you both have a chance to prepare, and bring a clear and concise discussion to the table. If you adopt a collaborative approach rather than a black-versus-white attitude, it can seem more like a team meeting than a confrontation. You may even discover the issue wasn't that important once it's cooled.

Set a rule to never argue where you sleep. Bedrooms are sacred spaces, and often the only place where you and your partner can find a little couple's privacy in your home. This is not where to bring your arguments so the kids or the neighbors don't hear.

If you have a particularly bad argument in your bedroom, you could remember it for the rest of your days together — it may be a long time before you get a peaceful night's rest. Negative energy is real, whether you acknowledge it or not, and bad memories in what should be a peaceful place could haunt your relationship. I have always had the rule to never go to bed angry, and it's made a big difference over the years in my personal happiness.

Instead, choose a neutral, quiet environment away from the TV and the laptop — and leave your phones in the other room. Make eye contact, engage, and use non-threatening and non-defensive body postures (if your mouth is agreeing and your arms are crossed in front of you, you're not taking it in). If you do have kids or neighbors, do your very best to wait until they're at school or asleep, or get out of the house completely for an important discussion.

Managing the family

Stressed teenagers aren't the only issue with family life—although they may be factoring in your list pretty high right now. Coping with the everyday craziness of living with any family, big or small, is more than enough to fill a hundred thousand very good books written by experts on the subject, so here I'll be brief.

A NutriGlamorous life is all about balance, and no two families are the same. Dynamics will be extremely different from household to household. If you always feel like you're struggling to get away, or even stop yourself thinking about all you have to do for your family... take a deep breath. I can't tell you how many clients have wailed to me, "I can't find five minutes to myself!" This is your life, and you need to ask yourself what is wrong. Have you taken on too much responsibility? Are outside forces truly beyond your control intervening in ways you can't change? Or is there another reason you feel overwhelmed?

Remember this: love first.

If you feel like you're drowning in chores, doing everything yourself, and you hate the resentment bubbling beneath the surface when you hear yet another voice yell "Mom!"... love yourself enough to delegate some chores, and trust that your family loves you back and will take them on.

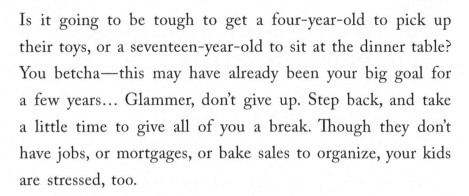

Is it going to be tough to get a four-year-old to pick up their toys, or a seventeen-year-old to sit at the dinner table? You betcha—this may have already been your big goal for a few years... Glammer, don't give up. Step back, and take a little time to give all of you a break. Though they don't have jobs, or mortgages, or bake sales to organize, your kids are stressed, too.

When you set better boundaries, your kids will respond better. When you respect yourself, your family will sense it and shift accordingly. You'll know when it's time to regroup. Reorganize. Research those reward charts on Pinterest, find someone who "gets it" when you need a freaking break already, and raise your kids with whatever your version is of love, discipline, and fun. Just like everyone else, you can't change them, you can only change you. When you change, they will miraculously develop new behaviors you could never get them to achieve by being pushy or shouting.

If you need help, get it. Family counseling may be in order, or some of those hundred thousand books. Remember, if it feels too big for you, it's not your fault. It's your job to be the mom and reach out, for everyone's sake as well as your own.

Identifying and dumping toxic relationships

Maybe your playground battles aren't over.

Maybe there's a mom at the school gates who gives you a sick feeling in your stomach when you spot her Beautycon ways. Or a co-worker who'll ruin your day with one sentence. Or your supposed BFF, whose caller ID on your phone makes you instantly want to hide.

There's a lot of talk about environmental toxins — one that is extremely harmful in your environment is a poisonous friendship.

You know you have a toxic relationship with someone because you'll feel it in your gut: it usually manifests as a sinking feeling, low thunder of dread or just a haze of sadness. It comes on when they're nearby, physically or in your thoughts.

Toxic people often use it as a tool. They can be experts in gaslighting (making you feel like you are the problem), demolition experts of self-esteem, and haters of everything NutriGlam—because they don't understand it. They are often so imbalanced, they cannot stand to see anyone else happy and rocking their lives, so they tear them down. Be careful, Glammer.

If you know a deliberately toxic person, first remove yourself from their sphere of influence. Cut ties, cancel lunch, get out of the room—give yourself space to gather your resistance. It will take effort to break away for good: this is because deliberately toxic people specialize in making you think you need them, that you're worthless, or you're imagining things.

If you think you are being physically or mentally abused, put down this book right now. Run, don't walk, to call someone you trust who is outside the situation: your local women's shelter, the Samaritans, or (if a crime has been committed) the police. You aren't alone, and things will be so much better without them, believe me. Once you just get away for a while, it's like waking up from a bad dream. Remember, safe equals stuck, and women have stayed in bad relationships until they were killed because, on some level, they were afraid that what they didn't know wasn't safe. Don't let your stuckness suffocate your dreams.

Just as draining, damaging, and toxic, are those so-called friends who don't even realize how manipulative they are. You will have to cut them loose—for your own sanity.

You know the ones—like the friend who only messages with tragic news or a big drama. She's blowing it out of proportion, you mutter under your breath, or she's stirred it up herself. Then you tell yourself off for thinking unkind thoughts.

It's not her fault Husband #3 left her, or her car needs fixing or rent's due yet again, or her terrible boss gave her another warning... or is it?

Lookit—bad, even terrible, luck happens for sure. Bad things can happen to good people, and fate may be cruel. Unfortunately, some individuals repeat bad patterns as if they're knitting a 2-ply sweater... over, and over, and over.

Stop picking up what they are putting down.

This goes for family, too. It's especially hard if you come from a big, close, strained or blended one. Toxic grown-ups should be dealt with in a grown-up way; if you don't need to ask their permission to stay up late, why are you acting like they run your life? Respect shared ties and experiences, of course—it's just who appointed you the family representative to listen to Aunt Doris talk incessantly about her medical issues? Whether a recent funeral has spawned an ugly fight between your siblings, or your parents refuse to accept that you are now in a same-sex relationship, the graceful, self-caring thing to do is take a Time Out and break up, at least for now.

The best—and sometimes hardest—path is always honesty. Tell them how their conversations make you feel, and point out specific examples where they've come across as uncaring, manipulative or nasty.

How they react will tell you what you need to do next.

Some people will make you their latest drama—they feel betrayed, how could you, you must hate them, etc. They may talk behind your back and tell other people you've been mean. Those shared friends may unite and call you name (in which case, they're most likely just as toxic). Or they might lend a sympathetic ear, secretly wishing they had the guts to tell your noxious friend or relative where to go, just like you

did. In either case, don't worry: either you'll be glad more Beautycons revealed themselves, or gradually your true friends will follow your lead and also abandon the bad apple, thereby improving everyone's lives.

Some people truly have no idea they've fallen prey to negative habits. They may apologize immediately, or go into a sulk —it's important to live up to your promise of breaking off contact. Let them come back later, when they're ready to accept where you are now. If they do, wonderful; you've strengthened your resolve, helped someone else, and strengthened a friendship. If they don't? Buh-bye, Beautycon!

Social media for good, not for evil

Social media is the store that's always open—and the main currency is love.

Little heart symbols, Likes, Follows, lots of selfies, secret stalking and furtive direct messages… it's about love and friendship, and also jealousy and passion, whether you vehemently disagree or are in sync with the issue. Even when you think you're just logging on for a couple of minutes to check the your news feed, the stakes are high.

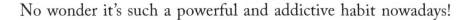

No wonder it's such a powerful and addictive habit nowadays!

You might be a self-confessed addict or staunchly resistant to even buying a smartphone (if you still have a Blackberry, you're not alone). Just remember, social media is, at its core, simply a way of staying in touch.

It's up to you—not corporations, not tech giants, not your friends or your family—to use it to lift up your life, instead of dragging you down.

Used NutriGlamorously, social media is enriching, expansive, and wonderful. Use it to discover new ideas and new friends, or explore old dreams and reconnect with lost relationships.

There's only one thing you need to remember: it's your choice.

Social media is an environment you create. Inundated with messages and tweets and requests? Slow down and remember you choose how often you are online. Hate seeing someone's posts? Unfriend them! Feel bad every time you see an Instagram diva strutting her stuff on the streets of Barcelona? Unfollow! No one gets a notice that someone has unfriended them, so what are you waiting for?

Glammer, it's so worth it.

Let's remodel our feeds, clear out the clutter and experience social media minimalism—it's time to clean house.

Did you know you can nearly always hide certain topics, feeds and people from your timeline? Often, you can simply put someone on 'mute' while you stay friends with them: they will still never know [10]. Most people won't notice if you unfollow them completely. Turn off every notification, and move your social media apps to the second page on your smartphone; reserve the prime real estate for podcasts, eBooks, productivity apps, or games you enjoy.

And if you can't mute, tidy up or otherwise edit to limit negative influences? Delete. Extinguish your profile, and never install the app again; you probably won't even miss it. I once left an online Harry Potter group that I loved, because I was spending a half-hour of my day in there, every day. It felt fun, and safe. It was also not a priority and it was a total time suck. Whether it's a Facebook group you would just miss too much or the 3,000th level of Candy Crush, if you just can't bear to give it up, use it as a way to reward yourself for an important task you complete, and set a timer on your phone to make sure you only do it for the length of time you choose.

Now... there's an elephant in the room we need to talk about: news and world events.

It can be terrifying out there, and whether you meant to or not, you've probably read or watched CNN and the New York Times and the BBC (and Fox News and for sure Breitbart) more in the past month than you used to in a year: sponsored videos, timeline posts, headlines... disasters, terrorism or politics are more in front of us than ever, not to mention a once-in-a-century pandemic.

Shared by your friends, or simply popping up as an ad, the news industry is capitalizing on the craziness of the 24-hour news cycle to get headlines shared, articles read, and controversy stirred up... whether the story is truly important, or even true.

How much do you really need to know? How much does political strife affect your day-to-day activities, or hearing about a terrible earthquake help you unwind after a long day? You don't have to ignore world events—just don't invite sadness and terror into your life without good reason.

Unfollow the news. If something truly important happens, you'll hear about it. Designate a friend who is addicted to the news to tell you if something happens that will affect you or your loved ones. The news is based on fear — that's why the headline reads:

Brazen Bank Robber Terrorizes Teller By Waving Around Loaded Gun (which YES, was an actual headline I found)

and not:

No One Harmed During Minor Bank Robbery

That fear seeps into your psyche and causes you to have a constant low hum of danger, which can affect everything from your well-being to the likelihood of inflammation in your body. [11]

I hope it goes without saying you should always donate to causes you believe in and raise awareness when you can—from a place of love, not a place of fear. (See the *Give* chapter for more on this)

All of these suggestions are about how to bring more love into your life. More peace, more joy. What can you do to allow love to flow? Consider that alllllllll your tiny little changes and new actions can add up, eventually (if you will allow it) to a life you always wanted to live and maybe never even thought was possible. It all starts with loving yourself. Pick the shifts in this book (the behaviors, the new habits, the choices you feel like you want) and start implementing, one at a time. Celebrate your new ways to show yourself that you deserve and are choosing self-care and self-love.

"Ego says, 'once everything falls into place, I'll have peace.' Spirit says, 'find your peace, and then everything will fall into place.'"

—Marianne Williamson

Breathe

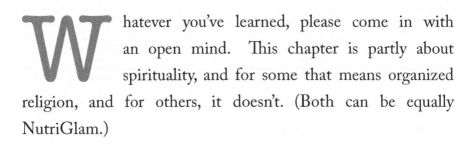

Whatever you've learned, please come in with an open mind. This chapter is partly about spirituality, and for some that means organized religion, and for others, it doesn't. (Both can be equally NutriGlam.)

Enjoy your spirituality in any way you please, pray to whomever or whatever you feel drawn to—your spirituality is your choice. It exists to help you find purpose, soothe and rejuvenate you, and, no matter how it's being wielded, not to be used as a weapon.

At the core of every Beautycon is a deep wound that compels them to push, pull or guilt others into their way of life: unfortunately, organized religion can be used as a tool by even well-meaning people to preach intolerance and turn us against eacg another. If you find yourself in the company of religious people who have hateful-sounding beliefs, love them right where they are, just don't join them in divisiveness.

I had a friend who was a born-again Christian, whereas I'm spiritual pantheist — I believe everything and everyone is part of God. After I complained about someone's religious sniping, she asked me what the difference was between their religious intolerance for others and my intolerance of their beliefs. I thought about this really profound question. My answer was: my belief means everyone wins. Atheist or

Ultra-Christian, Muslim or Jew — everybody has a reason, a purpose, and is entitled to their own opinions. No one is "not getting into Heaven" just because they don't believe what I believe. Unfortunately, my friend and I had a terrible falling out, because she eventually turned out to be a terrible Beautycon! Yet I never forgot that beautiful lesson.

Tolerance is about listening, creating a safe space for everyone to air their opinions without risk of harm. You can create that space by silently responding to every hateful thing they say with a silent, positive thought. Every time they make you uncomfortable, you can choose to meet that feeling with tolerance and protect your calm.

Wars are fought and nations have fallen because this can be really, really hard.

Imagine a religious person is telling you that someone you love—or you—should be punished for their actions or beliefs. While you listen, you cannot get heated or play their games; sometimes, it's best not to even argue. Think of the flowers outside, or that a stranger smiled at you that afternoon, think of your friend and connect with your deepest belief that their—or your—path is powerful, and find sympathy for this close-minded person. All you need to calmly say is, "I agree to disagree."

Beautycons will fight desperately to break you down, get you to concede a point or simply humiliate you; you don't even

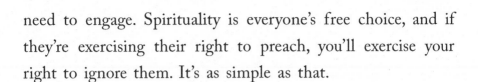

need to engage. Spirituality is everyone's free choice, and if they're exercising their right to preach, you'll exercise your right to ignore them. It's as simple as that.

How to reconnect with your higher power

I think everyone believes in a higher power: God or science. No matter how we look at it, we humans are adrift in a vast sea we know nothing about, with new discoveries every single day changing our perceptions of our world and sending us off on new paths—whether you call it God, fate, luck, or unseen forces, nearly everyone will agree our daily lives are influenced by something bigger than we are and beyond our control. Spirituality is based on the notion that engaging with these higher powers, inviting them into our ordinary lives and communicating with them, makes us happy and improves emotional intelligence.

If you believe in God, this means getting to know Him, Her, or It and finding out what kind of plan God has in store. You might call God by one of its other names: Spirit, or the Universe, Creator, or (as they do in 12-step) Higher Power — or even its nickname, HP.

If you believe in science, religious feelings may simply be a function of the brain to ensure release of a concoction of

chemicals like serotonin and other "feel good" hormones—that sounds pretty beautiful to me anyway! Belief in science is also a belief in something greater than yourself. You can call it nature, or Unseen Forces (like Change Management expert Price Pritchett), or the Field of Possibility (like best-selling author Pam Grout), or just make up your own name for it.

To connect with your own higher power, sit very still when you have at least fifteen minutes of spare time, and be as quiet as you can. Silence may be best, or a soundtrack of rushing water, bells, waves, or rain. If you've never done this before, your thoughts will start buzzing around like an interstate at rush hour—no sooner than you've thought one thought, you'll already

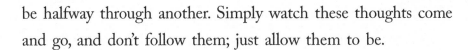

be halfway through another. Simply watch these thoughts come and go, and don't follow them; just allow them to be.

If you're new at this, your thought train may keep chugging right along:

Gotta pick up the package, dentist at two, kitchen counter still a mess, my leg is itchy, if I scratch does that mean I have to start again, why am I thinking so much, gotta keep thoughts quiet, stay still, wow this is boring, I can't do this, how much longer, wonder what's for dinner...

Don't worry, it's totally normal! Treat your mind like a chattering friend: listen and just observe.

Sooner or later, the voice will quiet. Or, those quick thoughts will turn to bigger questions and worries. When that happens, you'll notice your mood change slightly, good or bad. And underneath all that chatter, you may get a sense of deeper feelings and intuition.

Let them guide you.

Maybe they're saying, *I know God is supposed to be there, I just feel like I've lost Him/Her/It.* Or, *I don't think I believe in anything at all, and I'm okay with that. I wish others would stop pressuring me.* Or, *I really want to check out pantheism/Buddhism/ automatic writing. I feel drawn to new things.* Or, *I feel like I need different faiths for different times in my life—I don't want to have just one.*

The most beautiful thing about your higher power is that it's always with you, whether you're aware of it or not, whether you believe in it or not. You might think of it as your intuition or a gut feeling — it's all good. This means if you feel lost, you can find yourself, and if you feel you're searching in a desert, an oasis is always right around the corner; the journey to becoming 'spiritual' is just as important. In fact, for many faiths, this is actually the point: we're all imperfect, always searching, and even people who seem like 'experts' are still learning, me included. Always. The important thing is that you choose what works for you — the expression is "let the road rise up to meet you" and it's never more important than when you are considering something this personal.

Why spirituality doesn't necessarily mean religion

Having a church is a wonderful experience, as you've joined a ready-made community united in spreading love and reassurance to others. Let's face it, most of you don't have much in common, apart from maybe living in the same neighborhood; what an easy way to get together and discover new friendships!

Now what if you don't feel drawn to any particular faith, or the thought of organized religion makes you feel

uncomfortable? Don't worry—spirituality is bigger than that. Though you may not be able to put a name to your beliefs, they still believe in you.

Spirituality is two parts philosophy, one part faith, and a healthy dose of balance. Mix them all together as you prefer—with an annual retreat, a daily mantra, prayer, walking around the block, or any other ritual that you feel called

to. As long as it expands your mind beyond your mundane worries, helps you contemplate what things mean to you, or shows you deeper patterns and influences in your life, it 'qualifies' as spiritual. It's simply the practice of reaching a little further, strengthening our emotional muscles, and opening our minds to greater meaning [12].

How to find the right spiritual practice for you

It's pretty simple—listen to your inner voice, then do what it says! Sit quietly more often, learn to use mala beads, check out a new church, or read and explore as many new ideas as you can. The NutriGlamorous journey is all about recognizing you as an individual; how do you know what's right for you unless you sample it first?

Know that a big part of being spiritual is about loving the journey. Reverend Michael Beckwith, minister of the Agape International Spiritual Center, says "We are all one breath away from enlightenment; the question is, which breath?" We are all on the same journey, just different paths to get there — how (and how quickly) you walk yours is up to you.

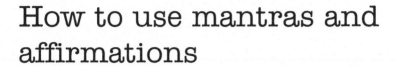

How to use mantras and affirmations

One of the most fascinating parts about how we humans participate in religion is that many of our faiths include the same ingredients: bathing in cleansing water, uplifting chants, hymns, mantras or scents.

This is a lovely awareness, because these practices connect us across time, space and different faiths—and it means that they work, at least for most of us. Since there's no copyright on religion, you can feel free to pick and choose what feels right for you.

Mantras and affirmations have been proven to help with issues such as weight loss, spirituality, good habits and reducing stress [13]. They function by focusing the mind on the meaning of the mantra, releasing tension with repetition, and—when spoken aloud—acting as a soothing voice to relax the listener and send out a positive vibration of sound.

Mantras are a more spiritual word or phrase, which is spoken, thought or chanted to relax the mind into a meditative state. You can use your preferred name for Spirit, a word which connects you with a sense of peace, such as Love or Joy, or even just a pleasing combination of sounds. 'OM' is the

sound of creation, a beloved mantra used all over the world [13, 14].

An affirmation often has a more tangible 'goal' in mind: meant to reassure, enlighten, and reaffirm, and if you haven't achieved the thing, to claim it now. I AM is also the sound of creation, since it calls the thing you desire into present tense. Phrases like 'I am success' and 'I am loved' make excellent affirmations, to write on a card and read multiple times a day, to speak aloud in front of the mirror or just think to yourself whenever you have a quiet moment.

It's not easy to come up with mantras and affirmations on your own, especially if you're not used to talking to yourself in a kind and caring way. So here are some powerful suggestions to get you started — read through them all twice, and whenever you need a pick-me-up. Daily, choose (at least) one that resonates for you: it makes you feel good, and you like it, and it feels real and true when you say it (or at least it feels like it could be real for you eventually). Keep this practice up and you'll soon get into a rhythm of loving, caring self-talk, and you'll be able to adopt one as your personal mantra or create your own:

1. I am the architect of my life; I build its foundation and choose its path.

2. Today, I am brimming with energy and overflowing with joy.

3. My body is healthy; my mind is brilliant; my soul is tranquil.

4. Today, I am turning all my thoughts positive and making better choices.

5. I have been gifted with endless talents which I will utilize today.

6. I forgive those who have harmed me in my past and peacefully detach from them.

7. A river of compassion washes away my anger and replaces it with love.

8. I am guided in my every step by a power that leads me towards my desires.

9. My relationships are becoming stronger, deeper, and more stable each day.

10. I already have the qualities I need to be as successful as I wish.

11. Creative energy surges through me and leads me to new and brilliant ideas.

12. Happiness is a choice that I base on my own accomplishments and the blessings I've been given.

13. My ability to conquer my challenges is limitless; my potential to succeed is infinite.

14. I am courageous and I can stand up for myself.

15. My thoughts are filled with positivity and I radiate prosperity.

16. Today, I abandon my old habits and take up new, more positive ones.

17. Money comes to me from sources known and unknown.

18. Many people look up to me and recognize my worth.

19. I am blessed with an incredible family and wonderful friends.

20. I acknowledge my own self-worth; my confidence is soaring.

21. Everything that is happening now is happening for my ultimate good.

22. I am growing; I am grateful for my growth.

23. My future is the projection of my dreams and my results are powerful.

24. My efforts are being supported by the Universe; everything is working to aid me.

25. I attract the best relationships for my highest and best good, and continue to call forth harmony.

26. I radiate beauty, charm, and grace.

27. I am in perfect health. Whatever my current condition appears to be, I affirm only health and wholeness for my body.

28. Obstacles are melting away; I am strong and in control.

29. I am grateful for all the money I have right now and all the abundance I am receiving.

30. I wake up today with strength in my heart and clarity in my mind.

31. Tomorrow doesn't exist yet, so I can create a better one with my powerful new thoughts.

32. I am at peace with all that has happened, is happening, and will happen.

33. I receive beautifully and create a giving loop for my receiving.

34. My nature is spiritual, and I am a spiritual being.

35. The rest of my life is just beginning.

The following mantras are just for work — if you have your own business, or you'd like a more fulfilling job:

1. My business is growing, expanding, and thriving.

2. I attract the perfect clients, and the perfect people to work with in my business.

3. I manage my money beautifully and I am grateful for my financial success.

4. I have my ideal employment and I love my work.

5. I am grateful to be well-employed and to have work I enjoy.

6. I deserve to be employed and paid well for my time, efforts, and ideas. Each day, I am closer to finding the perfect job.

7. My work issues resolve themselves easily and I am a great team player.

8. Opportunities come to me effortlessly and I am open to more good in my business.

9. I experience my work in perfect balance with my personal life.

10. Gratefully, I allow my work to thrive and to support me.

How to practice self-care daily

Self-care is trending nowadays and many Beautycons have jumped on the bandwagon, preaching cups of tea and hot baths and 'five minutes to ourselves' at every moment.

Even the phrase 'self-care' has become overused; it's lost almost all meaning. How do you practice self-care? Typically,

it means activities that are pleasurable and preferably slightly healthy; you've heard most all the ideas... Take a long walk. Draw a bubbly bath. Drop the kids off at grandma's. Indulge in a breathwork class. Treat yo'self!

Perhaps you can't get over how selfish this seems, or it's frustrating that you just can't find the time to do this as often you want. Either way don't listen to Beautycons who try to tell you the 'right' way to perform this most personal task. If they've truly found something that works for them, that's great. Consider ideas like baths and tea and yoga retreats, then if something doesn't feel good to you—move on. Don't buy just because they're selling!

Self-care, for you, could be as simple as singing along to your favorite songs in the car. Or buying a caramel latte and really, really enjoying it with zero guilt. For me, one choice is having breakfast on my favorite set of dishes, which are hand-painted and make me smile every time I use them. Maybe you're one of the lucky few already practicing enough self-care—anything that comforts you, gives you peace, and brings you joy... that's the right idea.

For some, self-care is social—they love chatting with friends, organizing trips and volunteering. For others, being alone is self-care: reconnecting with their own interests and the quiet in their minds.

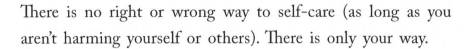

There is no right or wrong way to self-care (as long as you aren't harming yourself or others). There is only your way.

Unfortunately, for some of us, at least some of the time, self-care can be the hardest thing in the world.

It's because we're not being honest with either ourselves or (especially) others, about what we truly need. We need food, and air, and sleep, sure—and once our survival needs are met, we need time and space and love. We learn how to ask this of others, yet how many of us know how to give it to ourselves?

It might be that you've reached a point where you have to radically cut your commitments and practice self-care for your mental or physical health. In this case it's hardly 'indulgence;' it's a necessity. Self-care isn't always facial masks or Pilates. It can be healthful, nourishing food, exercise and getting back on track. Whatever is essential to keep yourself from falling apart.

Though the Beautycons on TV might be able to treat self-care as a luxury, for those of us who work very hard and don't have enough time to ourselves, it's vital: for us, self-care can be salad and space to concentrate. It's a run in the morning or a total reset. It's refusing to tolerate the status quo for one more second.

A woman called me once with a problem. A woman she had known in high school, a total Beautycon, had reared her head (because, of course the Universe will supply these

lessons over and over until we learn them). My client's question was — do I have the right to speak up? Do I have the right to say this isn't okay with me and ask for something different? She was essentially asking for the right to be heard, for the right to tell her truth. This is a strong, intelligent woman who was taught as a small child to grin and bear it, that family always comes first, to take one for the team. These are cliché now, of course, because we've all heard them so often.

As little girls, we are taught that if we are powerful, we are aggressive. If we are decisive, we are bitchy. If we want too much, we are demanding. A man once called me the most demanding woman in the world. At the time, I was offended. I went home and cried! Eventually, I realized: That as a badge of honor! I WANT to be the most demanding woman in the world!

Because, guess what? That's going to make me less demanding than about 40% of the men! Here's what men are told: be aggressive, be bold, be brave, stand on your own two feet, claim what you want. It's the natural birthright of men to be able to act like this. That's why we have this thing called a patriarchal society, which basically means that men run things, even things which perhaps should belong exclusively to women.

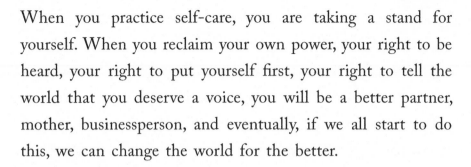

When you practice self-care, you are taking a stand for yourself. When you reclaim your own power, your right to be heard, your right to put yourself first, your right to tell the world that you deserve a voice, you will be a better partner, mother, businessperson, and eventually, if we all start to do this, we can change the world for the better.

Imagine that by putting yourself first, we can create a matriarchal society: one of cooperation, of building up your sisters (and yourself) instead of tearing them down. This is a place where you can say, *This is what I deserve! I have not made myself crazy because I forgot to take care of myself, or neglected myself so completely my body got sick and shut down, because, as usual, I was the last person on my to do list. By my learning that I have the right to tend to my own garden first, I have more produce to share with the rest of the world. I have more things to say that are important, I can give of my time to my children, to my partner, to my beloved, to my parents, to my community, to my planet, because I have already nurtured myself.*

Try putting yourself at the top of your never-ending to do list and you will find you accomplish more, and that you can do it with grace, without resentment, in better balance.

Are you settling for less than you deserve? Are you strangling some part of yourself? What are you giving up, that's not okay with you any longer?

Self-care is knowing when to put yourself first, above others, even though it seems uncomfortable. None of us is magically invincible all of a sudden, no matter how old we are or how much we get done in a day. If we burn out, we can't give 100% to our families, careers or any of our life's purpose. Recognize that self-care is a radical approach to healing the world, one person at a time—starting with ourselves.

"Earth does not belong to us; we belong to the Earth."

— Chief Seattle

Earth

You know the old saying, Save the Earth, we've only got one.

Earth is our home, and we are overall being lousy stewards. If the Earth were our back yards, it would be as if we had parties every night and never bothered to clean up after the guests left.

Our human instinct is to keep our nests cozy. The NutriGlamorous way is to extend that desire beyond our own front door, remembering that what we do can have far-reaching impacts on the other side of the globe. We can all agree Nature is a beautiful thing, and we should all probably be doing a little (or a lot) more to help her.

Headlines scream at us: "Oceans clogged with plastic!" "Bees are dying!" "Ice caps are melting!" "More hurricanes on the way!" And now we've had a global pandemic that has shut everything down. It's all so terrifying, you'd be forgiven for jumping under the sheets and not coming out until we all have homes on Mars. Yet we are starting to see that things don't have to stay that way.

My dad had cataract surgery, and the next day, when the doctor took the bandage off his eye, my father started to cry. "Dad, what's the matter?" I asked.

He looked at me, smiling. "Nothing's wrong... I can see white again!" His eyes had yellowed slowly over time until

he could no longer see true. Yet overnight, the change was obvious.

That's where we are right now, with the planetary shifts our isolation has revealed. The smog has cleared in LA and China, thanks to the lack of traffic and factories being closed. The waters of the Caribbean are getting a chance to recover from 10 million annual cruise ship tourists. In India, 60 million turtle babies are born on just two beaches in a single season because we aren't there to poach them... or watch them. It's all happened in a matter of weeks and months, and now we can no longer avoid climate change because it's suddenly obvious that we humans are changing the environment.

Since you're only one person, what can you do? Pioneering scientist Margaret Mead said, "Never doubt that a small group of thoughtful, committed citizens can change the world; indeed, it's the only thing that ever has." You only need to do one person's work to help heal the natural world a little.

And if you're a mom, partner to a busy worker, or just someone who appreciates a gleaming countertop, you can start by enjoying a clean, well-functioning, organized home.

You don't need to turn your backyard into a recycling plant, install a soil toilet or even give up your favorite scented candles—the everyday steps you can take are even smaller. Don't feel like you have to do everything, especially all at

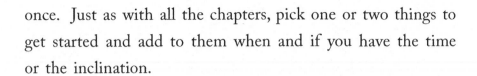

once. Just as with all the chapters, pick one or two things to get started and add to them when and if you have the time or the inclination.

One more important note: If you are emotionally sensitive, and you are feeling depressed because of the bushfires in Australia or the latest war being started on multiple fronts, please remember your mental hygiene. Sip the news, don't gulp it down just because everyone else does. Take a big step back from social media, avoid the nightly news, do what it takes to keep your energy clean. You make wish to read a news digest that has no images, listen to just the headlines on your smart device, or stop following certain groups on Facebook. Remember that you can take action and enact changes without immersing yourself in the daily crazytown of the 24-hour news cycle.

The environment at home

The biggest environmental impact of your home is your utilities. Consider your electricity, water and heating bills; it's vital that you don't use more than you need, both for a cleaner environment and more money in your pocket [15]. Here are some easy changes you can make.

Don't heat an empty house. During the winter, turn down your heat and if you start to feel chilly, put on a sweater

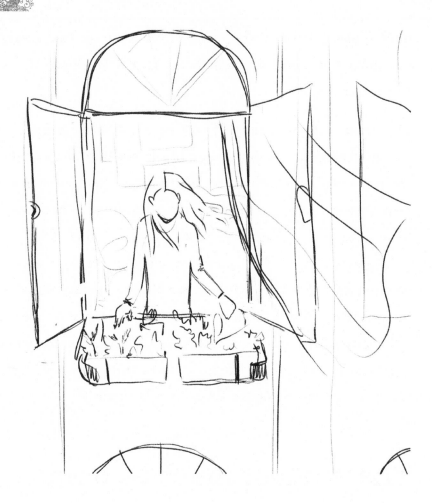

or a pair of cozy socks before your adjust your thermostat. Unless you live in Florida, January isn't designated T-shirt weather inside your home. Considering upgrading to a smart thermostat if you can, which will adjust itself based on your habits and movement.

Always turn your computer and monitor, or laptop, off when you're done using it. Consider unplugging it—even when it's

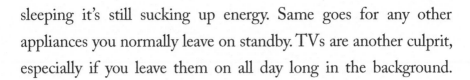

sleeping it's still sucking up energy. Same goes for any other appliances you normally leave on standby. TVs are another culprit, especially if you leave them on all day long in the background.

Next, cut down on the amount of paper moving in and out of your home. Put a sign in your mailbox requesting that no junk mail be delivered (and get off those mailing lists, too), switch to online/paperless billing, and cancel newspaper and magazine subscriptions in favor of digital versions. Take old magazines to the recycling center, or an assisted living facility for them to read. Less clutter for you, and fewer trees will be cut down!

Rechargeable batteries are a great solution for home gadgets you can't do without; the electricity you use charging them has nowhere near as large a carbon footprint as creating, delivering, and disposing of those normal batteries. While you switch, recycle your old batteries at the supermarket or recycling center.

Cut down on plastic bag waste by reusing your bags, taking them back to the store, or stop using them altogether. Buy (or make) your own fabric bags to carry your groceries. Some states have already outlawed single use plastic bags, and others will follow, so get ahead of this trend.

Got a little one? According to one study, you'll use over 4,000 diapers before your baby is potty-trained, and an average of 5,000 nappies in total. This all adds up to a massive 400,000

tons of waste every year—that's 2–3% of all household waste! This is why many environmentally conscious parents buy reusable diapers, which are often made of fabric that can be tossed in the laundry after they're used. However, by washing and drying them, you will generate the same amount of carbon emissions as it takes to manufacture the same amount of throwaway diapers. So use an eco-friendly washing machine, and save the diapers for your next child or pass them on to a new mom. This way, you could slash that harm to the environment by about 40%! [16]

How to compost

If you love gardening, you can start using your food waste to grow some vegetables or flowers. This gives you an eco-friendly double whammy —you're reusing waste, and growing extra plants! There are also easy (and non-messy) self-contained bins, which is great if you have a big green thumb and only a small balcony. If you want to spend some bucks and keep your hands clean, this is the way to go!! If, on the other hand, you want to watch all your organic waste turn itself into rich earth, and get some great exercise at the same time, read on!

Start by gathering food waste and other natural trash around your home to begin your composting. Vegetable peelings, old

newspapers, scraps of cotton and yarn, coffee grounds, tea leaves, dryer lint, weeds, pine needles (that old Christmas tree!), dead leaves, sawdust and even fireplace ash can all be composted. Also, chicken and rabbit manure make excellent compost fodder; just beware of composting cat litter. You can only compost wood pellet litter, and the meat proteins in your cat's scat may carry diseases. If you do decide to compost it, use only on flowerbeds where children don't play, and never to grow vegetables. The rule is, herbivores are good, and poop from any meat-eating animal is out!

Also, never put meat or dairy leftovers into a compost pile. The proteins will attract flies and won't break down properly. Dispose of these somewhere else! You can put eggshells on the compost heap if you bake them first, to neutralize the protein in the egg residue. Or just throw them out with the meat scraps. Citrus is also a no-no, since it can kill beneficial earthworms.

A good way to start your compost pile is on bare earth, if you can. This allows worms and other good garden beasties to aerate the compost and carry over to your garden beds. If you haven't got enough space, you can compost in an aerated storage box or bin, or compost straight into vegetable beds with a rotation system, like this: you use three out of four, and the fourth to age your compost. The next year, when the crop is over, rotate out and use the fresh compost to grow

veggies in the super rich soil while using a different bed to compost. You can even compost in the bottom of flower pots or window boxes.

To start your compost pile, lay down some twigs or straw a few inches deep. This lets excess liquid drain into the soil and encourages air circulation (you want the material to rot, nicely—a soggy pile is a stinky pile). Add your compostables in layers, alternating moist ingredients such as food scraps, seaweed and coffee grounds, with dry materials like leaves, sawdust and cardboard. Add a good source of nitrogen such as manure or silage to 'activate' the compost pile and speed up the process [17].

If you live in a really dry climate, you'll want to occasionally water the compost heap to keep it moist, otherwise it will just mummify. (Mmm... mummified garbage. No thank you!!) Every couple of weeks, give the pile a quick turn with a pitchfork or shovel to circulate oxygen deep within the layers and get some awesome exercise! You may notice your compost pile actually steaming in cold weather—this is the rotting process creating a ton of energy! The best part about a compost pile is simply adding the materials on top when you need to get rid of them. No more slimy garbage spilling onto the curb—and you can rest assured your leftovers are going to work, feeding the earth sooner rather than later.

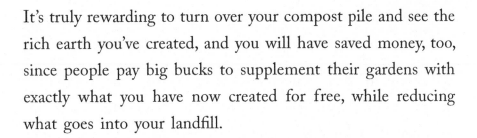

It's truly rewarding to turn over your compost pile and see the rich earth you've created, and you will have saved money, too, since people pay big bucks to supplement their gardens with exactly what you have now created for free, while reducing what goes into your landfill.

Make do and mend

The phrase 'make do and mend' comes from a pamphlet issued by the British Ministry of Information during World War II [19]. It was intended to provide women with useful tips on how to be both thrifty and fashionable while they dealt with harsh rationing and their menfolk serving overseas. Readers got tips such as stitching patches of pretty material over holes in their garments, unraveling old sweaters and using the yarn to re-knit more modern styles, and altering men's clothes to fit and flatter their shapes. Women had to work in factories and help out with the war effort, and they couldn't do that as practically in skirts—so altering and recycling their husband's old pants became as much a fashion movement as a social one!

To reduce your carbon footprint even further, it's a great idea to learn the skills you need to repair clothes, small items and even furniture when they get broken. This is a great way to

help out Mother Nature, learn a new hobby and save money, and it also has a deeper purpose: connecting us with our stuff.

So often in this consumer-centric world, we accumulate things at an alarming rate, never really knowing exactly all we own. By taking the time and effort to interact with our things, repair them and bring them back to life, we're making the conscious decision to value our possessions beyond what our throwaway culture tells us.

Mending and repairing is a very therapeutic process, so it can contribute to your journey as a Glammer on many more levels than one!

You can take local sewing or crochet classes, educate yourself with YouTube tutorials, or ask a friend or relative — it turns out I have several friends who knit and crochet for fun and meditation!

Creating your own clothes is a fun and rewarding pursuit—and fabrics don't have to be expensive. Search thrift stores for interesting vintage prints, or old sheets: more than enough material for a dress, and it only costs you a few dollars!

Speaking of thrift shops, it was NutriGlam to go second-hand shopping years before Macklemore & Lewis made it a #1 song. Some of my very favorite wardrobe pieces are vintage. It's a great way to get designer pieces at a fraction of the price, too. If you aren't the Goodwill or Salvation Army type,

consider consignment shops. You can often find clothes that have been worn once, or never! My latest find was shopping in a sweet rural town in the deep South. At a boutique that was half antiques and half consignment clothing, I stumbled upon a vintage Nicole Miller dress with the tags still on. It cost $20 and looks like a million bucks! I should point out that it was from the 1980s, which I guess makes me vintage, too!

The environment at work

When you're working from home in your own office, keep both a trash can and a recycling bin in your space so you aren't tempted to tell yourself you'll separate the garbage once a week.

If you love scented candles or plug-in air fresheners, make sure to find ones with natural ingredients and scents — a quick internet search turns up multiple studies that show health concerns linked to the chemicals in many commercial brands.

When you can't control your office environment, it can be deflating to come to a less-than-NutriGlam workplace every day and put up with Styrofoam cups and no recycling.

That said, there's a ton of ways you can start making your job a little more green—and you may find better friendships emerge when you get co-workers on board, too!

First of all, consult your boss. She or he will be able to listen to your concerns, and may not realize that incentives exist for companies wanting to go green. Your employer could save money on re-use or get tax breaks, and you can be the one to bring the good news.

Donating used goods is tax-deductible, and keeps waste out of landfills. Computers, furniture, and unwanted items can all be donated for a deduction of the fair market value of

the items, or what they'd sell for in their current condition. Businesses can also get tax credits for specific energy-saving investments, such as in solar and wind technology [18].

Encourage the habit of switching off all computers at the end of day, and turn on energy saving modes on all computers and monitors. Do some final checks at the end of your day, such as making sure all of the office lights, faxes and copiers, coffee machines and microwaves are turned off and, if possible, unplugged. Did you know sockets 'leak' power when electronics are left plugged in? Take it off standby mode, and unplug it at the wall, or better yet, use a power strip so you can flip a switch and turn everything off. If you have sockets that shut off, power them down at the wall.

According to Duke Energy's Vampire Calculator, for every desktop computer that's off when not in use instead of sleeping, you'll save $25 a year, and every LCD monitor saves $1.30. Imagine how much we'd save if we all did that!

Instead of using Styrofoam or cardboard cups at the coffee machine, suggest bringing in your own mugs or insulated cups. And why not suggest Meat-Free Mondays? Animal product consumption is one of the largest contributors to global warming, so suggest everyone become vegetarian, just for eight hours a week. Post fun recipes in the break room, share inspiration and favorite cooking tips—who knows, some of you might not even go back to steak and bacon!

How much printing do you have to do at the office? If you're in a business that prints everything, maybe it's time to make the switch to a digital system, especially with secure documents that also have to be shredded. Between a paid secure shredder service and the cost of paper, you might become your company's cost savings hero! Consider asking everyone to keep correspondence only in email, and to add an environmentally-friendly reminder in their signature, too.

When you work from home, using a digital contract app, switching to all LED lights, and adjusting your thermostat during the days can really add up! Please also make sure you recycle. One small bag of recycling weekly, all stacked up over 52 weeks, equals a big pile that you didn't contribute to a landfill. Because it's only you "in the office," small changes can make a big difference. Don't assume it's not important enough to bother with – and enjoy the feeling of doing your own small part in the world.

The environment of your life

There are many kinds of pollution. It's bad enough having noxious gasses seeping into our air; we also have to put up with noise, anger, and the divisiveness that has become our daily lives, all adding stressors that can have deep, lasting impact on

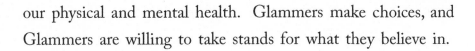

our physical and mental health. Glammers make choices, and Glammers are willing to take stands for what they believe in.

Anti-racism

This one's a no-brainer: don't be a racist. And no matter what your skin color, you probably just thought, "I'm not!" First of all it's now important to realize that not being racist means more than it did when I was growing up; today, it means speak up and speak out against hateful behavior and even careless words. That's why it's core NutriGlam to be anti-racism.

Racism came from the systemic and deliberate oppression of people who possess just a few cell layers that hold different amounts of melanin than the oppressors. It has a complex history that with underlying roots in a lot of money and deeply misguided thoughts of superiority. Today, racism can be a subtle form of bullying; people needing to feel better about themselves by believing they are better than others. Ironically, it makes them "thin-skinned," and rather than just letting everyone else live their lives, they have to belittle and bully them. Make no mistake; racism can kill, yet it can be an insidious culture of behavior that is perpetuated generation after generation.

If you've never faced racism or other discrimination, lucky you. However, that means you saw or heard it, and likely did nothing. If racial discrimination stopped tomorrow, within one generation, our children would no longer care about it because we would stop teaching them to hate people who looked or acted different. If you were raised to hate, or even to dislike or ignore, it's time for you to take the responsibility to fix it – get educated about what was left out of your school curriculum (a lot) and what you can do to help change the future.

We all have to watch our words more carefully, and pay more attention so we don't perpetuate racial stereotypes (even inadvertently). Not every Asian is smart, Black people don't all speak Ebonics, Jews aren't greedy with money, not all Latinos have great dance moves... whether it's a good stereotype or a bad one, it's still participating in a label that can cause racism. Don't hesitate to speak up for someone else who is being wronged; one day that wronged person may be you.

If this doesn't seem like it matters to you, I truly urge you to educate yourself about this important topic. Being NutriGlamorous means making a difference in your own corner of the world, and choosing your thoughts, your words, and your actions with care.

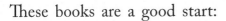

These books are a good start:

Ain't I A Woman: Black Women and Feminism, by Bell Hooks

I'm Not Dying With You Tonight, by Kimberly Jones

The New Jim Crow: Mass Incarceration in the Age of Colorblindness by Michelle Alexander

These are all written by women, and there are many other important books on racism to consider, so check out the longer list link in the endnotes. [20]

Politics

The biggest way we can impact our environment can have an important bearing on your life as a Glammer.

Politics is the single biggest instigator of change in nearly all walks of life, not least the climate. With global strife, hunger and poverty on the table, the environment often occurs only as an afterthought. That means it's up to us to lobby our politicians at home and abroad to make sure they do something about the issues we care about most. We have been seeing that recently in the Black Lives Matter movement, which has galvanized people even more than the civil rights movement of the 1960s, causing united protests

in countries around the world and, finally, some very overdue changes. Ordinary citizens are seeking to right the many wrongs done over hundreds of years of deeply rooted racial bias, recognizing that the status quo will no longer do; and unlike in times past, it's working quickly and effectively to implement new laws and new approaches to old problems. It's another example of how many people doing their small bit can lead up to big changes. Perhaps for the first time in our history, we are able to see that you *can* fight city hall. So if you want change, get involved.

First, know who your local legislators and politicians are. Find "my House Representative" online by searching those words—it's important to know who to get in touch with when you need to take action on an issue in your community.

Next, know how to make them listen. Writing on Twitter or Facebook usually doesn't work; their assistants just get paid to remove harassing posts, and they're not obligated to reply. Similarly, refrain from writing the President; whoever's in office gets a lot of mail! Write to your district office or state for a better result.

Want the best result? Pick up the phone.

If you call your representative at their district or state office, someone has to talk to you. It's impossible to read and reply to every letter they get, so a phone call is much more likely

to get a response. Assistants can use computer algorithms to batch letters based on subject and issue a standard reply; when you get someone on the phone, you've got their attention, even for just a moment. Script out what you are going to say. One or two sentences is best — mention your name, that you are a member of that district or state, and the issue you are concerned about. Ask the politician to take action, then remind them you vote.

Emily Ellsworth, who worked in Congress for six years, remembers when a radio host disagreed with the immigration policy and read out the office's phone number on air [21]. Thousands of people called in—jamming the phone lines, which exhausted the assistants and caused them to personally raise the issue to their seniors. Because of this action, steps were taken to address the public's concern.

Consider attending Town Hall meetings. This is where you can take the stage (these days sometimes virtually) and raise the problems closest to home, in front of local politicians who can actually do something about it. You can normally find a schedule of Town Hall meetings on your congress member's website. Attend a City Council meeting to get new insight into how your city works and the priorities steering important decision-makers and legislators.

If you're feeling drawn to it, you also may want to join a voting league or political organization. You can also volunteer at state, city and county party headquarters. They're always looking for volunteers, so they won't be hard to find. You'll most likely be put to work sending newsletters, taking part in online campaigns, attending rallies and events or even pounding the pavement in an effort to sway voters. Volunteering locally can connect you with neighbors and make you part of the local grassroots movements that are affecting change on the ground. This may give you a better

sense of your ability to make a difference (see the *Give* chapter for more specific ideas).

If you have kids in school, joining the PTA is an excellent way of volunteering and participating in how your school is run. Or you might want to get involved in your school board. Your school board is responsible for employing the superintendent, developing and adopting policies, curriculum, and the budget, overseeing facilities issues and adopting collective bargaining agreements—all of which impact your child, and thousands of others. Consult the state school boards association in your state to learn how to run for the school board.

Whatever your choices, I encourage you to stay out of the terribly divisive arguments that are constantly being fed to you on social media, and trickling down into family gatherings. A woman lamented after the 2016 Presidential election that the word "pussy" had suddenly become family dinner table conversation. Many clients have expressed their dismay that holiday events have become occasions for shouting matches with relatives and rifts created over politics.

If this sounds all too familiar, know that we could all use a return to kindness and civility. One of my favorite mantras is, "Everyone's always doing their best, even when that sucks." Having a calm political discussion with someone who opposes your views can be helpful. If it deteriorates into a fight, though, nothing will be accomplished and it's unlikely you

will change their viewpoint, especially once battle lines are drawn. So save your breath and your blood pressure.

Online, you can unfollow people on Facebook or snooze them until after the next election. You can click on the little close box on political ads to say you don't want to see them. You can avoid posting something divisive yourself. The best thing you can do for your world politically is to vote, and to encourage other like-minded folks to do the same. Everything else is just a word storm, and you, Glammer, have better things to do with your energy.

"*The law of increase in life is as mathematical a certainty in its operation as the law of gravity. And what this means for us is that getting rich is actually a science.*"

— Wallace Wattles

Money & Work

7

Most of us think that money energy is one thing, and regular energy (like the energy we harness for our electricity) are separate. What if they are not? What if they are the same thing? The truth is that energy is just energy. Einstein postulated that energy can never be created or destroyed, only transmuted. If you think you don't have good money energy, you may feel like you can't make a lot of money. Or that if you do, you will spend it. Or if you get a lot of money, you will lose it all. Or that bad things will happen to you if you get rich, because you know or have seen people who are wealthy, just not very nice. All of these things can block your natural flow, like having the law of gravity suspended.

One thing that can help is what I like to call Energy Transference: borrowing the energy of something you feel works really well in your world and applying it to something that does not. For example, I have really good parking karma. I am the person who can find the last parking spot in front of the mall on a snowy Christmas Eve, when the lot is filled with rabid shoppers who need "just one more thing." As I drive up to the front, somebody will just magically pull out in front of me. At first, I thought I noticed a parking pattern, yet it didn't always happen. After a while, as I focused on it, it started to happen a lot, to the point where I could see there was a repeatable expectation. It just felt right and easy, and I began

to trust it. *I have good parking karma,* I would tell myself, pleased with this thought as I got yet another awesome parking space. I was also broke. I had been broke for a long time, like ten years. By this time, the money pattern had repeated itself for so long, I just knew that I had terrible money karma. I was sure. This is the problem with any Beautycon myth — when we believe it, it's true. Don't want it to be true? You have to change your belief about it first.

I asked myself, *What if my parking karma and my money karma were the same thing? What if the certainty I felt, the surety that I was going to get that parking space* (as had been demonstrated to me many times) *was true about my money?* Which I believed to be a problem for me, no matter what I did. *Wouldn't that be cool?*

Guess what? Once I put those two things together and realized that my parking karma and my money karma WERE actually the same thing, it changed everything. It gave me the gift of understanding that energy was just energy. That money energy and regular energy were the same, and my belief was what had separated them.

Wallace Wattles, writing over a hundred years ago, said your money is a certainty (as do many other spiritual teachers). What if the law of gravity is as certain as the law that, if you focus on it in the right way, you have to get rich? This is

a golden opportunity for you to retool your thinking, to step out of the Beautycon myth that is perpetuated by almost the whole world, and to step into the actual Truth. Here's how, and to me, this is one of the secrets of the Universe:

There are myriad resources out there that tell you to focus on the positive, on the things that we desire. Think of the things you love and those that you desire as the Positive Tree. "If I had money (or love, or a better job, or a home I treasured, etc.) then I would be happy," is how most of us think of it.

Then we have our fears, our concerns, our things that keep us up at night. Our pain. Often when it comes to money, those things are all negative. "What if I don't have enough? What if I don't ever make any money again? What if I never get another client?" I can't tell you how many entrepreneurs I have worked with, their businesses in a slump, who would confess that their deepest fear was, "No one will EVER hire me again." All the stuff we are afraid of that hasn't happened, all the stuff that's happening to us that we don't like — that's our Negative Tree.

Every time you have a positive thought, you water your Positive Tree. Every time you have a negative thought, you water your Negative Tree. Usually, we spend so much time watering the Negative Tree, we kind of only give a little bit of attention to the Positive Tree. Now, what happens to something when we give it attention? It grows.

The expression is, where energy flows, results show. You can see it in an actual tree as well. You can see it in a plant in your home. If you don't water that plant, it withers, and eventually dies. So, what are you doing every time you're giving attention by watering the Negative Tree instead of the Positive Tree? You're pushing what you want away and you're bringing the thing you don't want closer to you.

It is really NutriGlamorous to feed the positive; it's also vital that you starve the negative. Literally, give it no attention so that it withers and dies. That is a huge key. If you knew it were certain you would get rich, if you knew it were certain that you would always have money, that Source/God would always supply your money, you wouldn't worry any more about it. You'd stop thinking about it. You'd stop watering the Negative Tree. And you'd start watering only the Positive Tree. Which would grow as the Negative Tree dies its stumpy little death.

Here is a great statement that will get your ego (which is afraid of change and wants you to stay exactly where you are now because it is safe) out of the way:

Tell yourself that God (or Spirit or whatever) is the CEO of your business, or if you work for someone else, that God is your boss. Never make another decision in your business again. Just keep turning the problem over to your CEO, ie.

your boss. Let them handle it. You will be surprised how often the solution comes to you in the shower, or as you're driving to work, or as you're falling asleep at night or waking up in the morning.

If you can get out of your own way, I can assure you that miracles will and do occur.

Your brain really wants to help. Your brain actually has wanted to help the entire time as it was telling you all these negative thoughts. It only wants to protect you. It would *love* to help. So next, invite your brain to get onboard. Have a conversation with it.

I know there's a book called *Kill Your Ego* (I sorta wanna kill the author) Because I don't believe in that at all. I believe that your ego is here to help and to support you. So, have a talk with your brain. *Hey, brain. I'm so grateful for you. It's just you're helping me the wrong way. I would like to encourage you to help me the right way, by reminding me immediately when I spend time in the negative, to stop and move toward the positive.*

When it comes to your money, it's time to be an excellent receiver as well as a good giver. You may be the kind of person who's great at giving gifts, yet has a very hard time receiving them. I once gave a gift to a dear friend. An big gift, something that was going to help her through a crisis.

The first thing she said, panicking, was, "Is it okay? Will you still have enough?"

I could energetically feel the contraction. I could feel her fear. I could feel that it wasn't okay to her for me to give. We expanded her back into YES right away (because I'm a coach, so that's what I do). The power for me to be able to just give and have somebody receive, welcoming, and have that receiving happen with open arms, that's very important. Because it creates a reciprocal flow. Be as good a receiver as you are a giver.

My favorite mantra is: "Yes, please, more, and thank you!" So, when something good happens, like more money, or a new client, or an unexpected check, or a new opportunity, you get to say:

1. **Yes, please**—This is you telling the Universe: Yes! I am so excited about this!

2. **More**—Please bring me some more of the same. Keep bringing it. I'm ready for it.

3. **And thank you!**—This is your gratitude, which makes everything more awesome.   I'm so grateful.

Yes, please, more and thank you!

All my mantras are very simple and easy to remember in a pinch, something your brain can hang its hat on to help when you are stuck in a situation. You want to remember

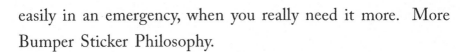

easily in an emergency, when you really need it more. More Bumper Sticker Philosophy.

Now onto work, and the money it brings us. A hundred years ago, the world of work looked very different, not least because it was a world from which women were, for the most part, excluded. Sure, we kept house, organized servants, and in the lower classes, cooked and cleaned and tended the garden and raised the children—and that sure is work! Back then women couldn't find 'traditional employment' unless they were nannies, nurses, or schoolteachers. Then they had to pick between marriage and a life of service.

Did you know that in the US, it wasn't until the late 1960s that a woman could have her own bank account without her father or her husband co-signing? Apparently, we weren't considered capable of managing our own money. Heck, it's only been about a hundred years since women got the vote in many countries! (In Saudi Arabia, women couldn't vote until 2015 and weren't allowed to drive until 2018!) [22]

Now, not only have we taken back the power to choose for ourselves what we want to do with our lives, the world of work has changed beyond recognition—there are many more types of jobs and unlimited ways to do them, and the glass ceiling is finally shattering as many of us learn to create our own economies by becoming business owners.

This means we've had to cram two hundred years of catch-up into about sixty years, carve out our own space in the world, plus deal with all the modern pressures of working life (learning new technologies, working overtime, sitting through boring meetings). Are you exhausted just thinking about it?

How to make work a better place

Given how much of our lives we spend there, we often hate being at the office. Isn't that a shame? Are there ways to make your workplace more NutriGlamorous, apart from the energy-saving tips I shared in the *Earth* chapter? It might be as simple as bringing in a few houseplants, or as complex as requesting a transfer. The question is, what can you do to stop merely tolerating your workspace? It deserves as much love and attention as you give your own home. After all, this is where you do your best work!

If you work from home, remember to keep that space a haven, too. Even if it's a closet, close the doors when you're not working. If you have a home office, look at the things in it and decide if they make you happy or they're just hanging out there because you don't have a place for them. If you

can't see your desk, take some Personal Me Time to declutter. More on that in the *Move* chapter.

If you don't work for yourself consider how much latitude you have: does your boss allow decorations, or even bringing pets to work? Can you move furniture, suggest a different location for the coffee machine, or move nearer to a window? Demonstrate your passion for making the work environment enjoyable for you and your co-workers. No smart boss will be

able to resist ideas for increasing productivity, especially if it's cheap and easy to do.

If all you have is your desk, treat it like a personal haven. If you aren't already enjoying your work for its own sake, compensate by keeping treats here that feel like indulgences or luxuries. Got a report due in an hour? Reward yourself afterwards by giving yourself a hand massage scented with your favorite essential oil. Stuck doing the filing when you are dreaming of the outdoors? Make it a bit more bearable with binaural beats audio on headphones (search for tons of freebies on YouTube by typing in "binaural beats" + keywords like "uplift," "joy," or "peace")

Of course, if you've got bigger workspace issues that are harder to control, it may take more effort. Bad bosses, water cooler time wasters, or soul-sucking clients can turn your perfect job into a total nightmare: and this time, unfollowing won't get rid of them. You can't block Beautycons in real life.

If this happens, be as civil as possible and set boundaries. Stop replying to go-nowhere or nit-picky emails. Set a rule that for lunch you're away from your desk. No one can ask you to work a full day without a break, so don't require it of yourself. Do not answer email at home, avoid run-ins in the kitchen, and if someone persists in bugging you, don't be afraid to ignore them or limit your exposure. You're here to do a job: remain professional, and don't put up with cruel behavior. Hold steady,

Glammer! Remember, you are worth it; you have value, and when you believe it, others will as well.

If things are truly untenable, consider contacting your HR department or lodging a formal complaint. You never know—other coworkers may be having issues with the person in question, and are too uncomfortable to speak up until you do. If things are more serious, please consider quitting or even taking legal action; is this job really more important than your tranquility?

We all sometimes worry that this is the only job or client we will ever get; when you stand in your own power, you will see that you are just as valuable at places or with clients that value you.

It's the 21st century—yet sexism in the workplace is still all too often a common occurrence, even with the Me, Too movement. This is one matter where action absolutely should be taken. Remember, being NutriGlam is all about honoring your best self; so you get to practice self-love, and also demand that respect from others.

If you think by playing the game you'll advance your career, get that corner office, they'll leave you alone, you'll feel better about yourself, or it's all just fun and games... sorry, sweetie, those are Beautycon lies.

Instead, the perpetrator will continue to demean other women, spread fear and shame, and worse—provide another terrible

example for others to follow in his footsteps. Don't put up with it, Glammer; break the chain.

And no, you don't need to have endured the ugliness of unwanted physical contact or slimy words in your ear to experience sexism. It can rear its ugly head in smaller acts such as men dominating the conversation, you getting paid a lesser amount for the exact same job, or being forced to wear uncomfortable heels as part of a 'dress code.' By speaking up and standing your ground, you will begin to effect change in small ways. Keep focusing on the results that you desire, and keep being grateful for the shifts you see.

Speaking of changes, let's talk about gossip. That's daily fodder for Beautycons, *not* for the NutriGlamorous, who care about more important things. Glammers are both more compassionate, and more productive. If you spend just 15 minutes of your work day talking about the other people at work, problem clients, or the current annoying situation (translation: gossiping) —over a single year, you will lose over 60 hours! That's a week and a half of work time! How many times have you asked yourself if you could have just five more minutes every day? Now you're getting a week and a half of your life back! How much more productive can you be? How much further can you get toward a big goal that you have set?

Choose awareness — see gossip happening and make an active choice not to participate. Choose mindfulness — you're making

a decision not to instigate gossip, too. These shifts will lift you up and allow you to focus more on the NutriGlam you.

Getting a better job

If your job is full of Beautycons, and you're not ready to strike out on your own, consider that the rules are changing for companies and that it is possible to find one that is both a conscious business and supportive of you. However, you may have to change the way you think about how to get hired.

According to Adweek, a staggering 92% of recruiters check social media to find high-quality candidates. That means before your charm and personality even had a chance to win them over, your potential employers were interviewing candidates they could find and feel they were already comfortable with. [23]

I'll presume you already have social media, so use it wisely. Untag any unflattering photos, and if every pic of you has a drink in hand, make sure to consider whether you are showing off your best side.

Of course a NutriGlam employer wants you to have a well-rounded life, so keep the silly faces at the county fair, and mementoes from your mountain climbing days, because who wants to work with anyone who doesn't like fun? Maybe they

will turn out to have something in common with you, and your ballet mom photos will spark a chord.

After you're done spring cleaning your social media, triple check that everything is up to date: your location, your job experience, and your skills. This is especially important on LinkedIn, which is like Facebook for business. If you don't have LinkedIn, you don't have job currency — if you're looking for work, or even new clients, it's important!

Start with a great profile picture—high quality, smiling, looking at the camera, just your head in the frame—and fill in all your relevant experience. Keep it brief, focused, engaging, and consider asking people who know your work to write a testimonial on LinkedIn.

When people contact you to make connections, always reply back, and start building up your network; leave your agenda at the door and concentrate on giving value. This is how people begin to associate you with the awesome work you do, and your great attitude. Feel free to tell people you talk to on private messages that you are looking for your next great opening. Just avoid posting it to the world if you are in a job where you don't want your current boss to know.

When you are looking for something, it's best to give first, before expecting help. Do you have a large network where you can support people? Do you have connections you can pass along?

Freelancing and Entrepreneurship

Consider this: your next employer could be sitting in your seat right now.

Working for yourself is increasingly common these days, especially with the digital economy creating myriad jobs we never had before. Fluent in Javascript? Great blog post writer? Know your way around business accounts? These are all jobs companies love to outsource, because it's cheaper, and there's no reason you can't be their freelancer.

Yes, Glammer, the life of a freelancer can be stressful. You've got no benefits at first, and you will need to budget your time as there's no one telling you when to clock off. Of course, the rewards are potentially huge: freedom, disposable income, and the feeling of total control over your earnings and your career.

Start by doing your research: first of all, do your skills match the freelance way of life? Could you do your job from home? If you write, design, code or consult, then probably yes. If your job requires large machinery, or a very specific type of environment... it might be best to consider other options.

After sheltering in place, many of us have a new idea of what it means to work from home, and can see the value of a 7-step

commute, and the kind of work and discipline required to get us there.

Creating your own job is a rewarding experience, and, as the digital economy grows, it may soon become the norm. I have worked with hundreds of entrepreneurs, and though there may be fear or wobbly bits, or internal programming that says you have to have a 9-to-5 for security, the truth is that starting your own business, alone or with a partner, can be incredibly rewarding. If you can create boundaries for yourself to start with, it's a powerful way to control both your

life and your income. You often can make a lot more money than you can as a salaried employee. And, no one will ever lay you off, which gives you the ultimate job security.

Growing Your Business

Once you are in business for yourself, remember to take time to work ON your business, not just in it. Schedule out a half-day a month, and a day a quarter, to vision and dream and to write those things down. Plan on an annual retreat in an exotic locale (check with your own accountant, because usually you can write it off) where you can look at the 65,000-foot view of your business without being bogged down in all the details.

Make sure your clients aren't claiming all your time and energy. If you start to feel resentful and overworked, that's not why you went into business, Glammer. Consider getting a coach or being really ruthless with yourself about whether you are being paid fairly for the work you are doing, and whether you need to raise your rates, or let go of clients who aren't in line with your mission.

What if it's not your clients? They may be great – you're just doing too much too often. All of us are given gifts and talents that we really own. You may be great with words, a natural marketer, a whiz with numbers, or a terrific salesperson.

You're unlikely to be all of the above at once, and even if you are, focus on the one or two things you feel are your "super powers" – the things only you can do in your business. Then give the rest away.

Not hiring someone because you think you have to do it all yourself is just wasting your valuable super powers, giving you the false belief that you are in control. If you have enough business just to get by, you'll have more business when you focus on the things only you can do. Wearing all the hats is not NutriGlam, it's exhausting. When you understand that by releasing control you can grow... now that's living!

Money, Honey

For some reason, Western society is deeply neglectful about teaching kids how to manage finances, so when we become adults and the world of mortgages, car payments and credit cards becomes ours, we often jump in without a clue as to what we are doing. You're not bad, or weird, or stupid for not wanting to put yourself on a budget or being unable to resist a sale, you're human.

The truth is, our money programming was put in place a long time ago. Almost without exception, in my experience, in our first decade of life. It was modeled by our parents

and the grown-ups in our lives, and we either behave exactly like those important role models now, or we are the exact opposite. I have clients who are repeating the same lousy programming as their parents, or who distanced themselves as far as possible to avoid those patterns, even when the patterns were good!

For you to truly step into being NutriGlamorous, just as in every other area of your life, it's vital that you make a decision to heal the old ways of behaving so you can live the life you came here to this planet to embody.

First, if you regularly ignore your finances or your own fears around money, it's time to stop that old way of being and choose something more supportive. As a Glammer, you may not be in the exact place you want to be financially, yet you understand that only you can make that difference in your own life.

Your next step is education. While it would have been awesome to learn these ideas in school, it's not too late now, and being NutriGlamorous also means being informed! Just as your weight issues are super simple though they may not feel easy (calories in minus calories out) your money issues operate on a similar principle: your income has to exceed your expenses. There are several excellent books that will give you straightforward, easy to follow systems, while helping to heal your money pains and programming. I am recommending

three of them here, that have all helped my clients and me over and over:

Secrets of the Millionaire Mind by T. Harv Ecker

You Are a Badass At Making Money by Jen Sincero

Profit First by Michael Michalowicz

Preview each of them online, then buy the one(s) that resonates with you.

Also, stop taking advice from people that have less money than you do, or the same amount. Or have had all their dreams shattered over and over. They may have their hearts in the right place and want to protect you; they will just succeed in making you feel like sitting in a dark corner of a bar, drinking cheap wine and feeling sorry for yourself.

If any of these issues sound familiar, it's time for you to stop feeling like your money has control over your life. Your money GIVES you control over your life, and once you take back that piece of your power, you will really feel NutriGlamorous!

"Giving is not just about making a donation. It's about making a difference."

— Kathy Calvin

Give

Whether you can give a little or a lot, it's an essential practice for any Glammer, and charity begins at home.

I used to think this adage meant several things: give at home, give from home, teach charity in the home. Now, I understand it means something even more powerful: give first to yourself and then you will have more to give others. Now that's NutriGlamorous!

Since we have already been giving to ourselves in the previous chapters, this one shows you how to give back. And since this is Planet NutriGlam, not the Hollywood red carpet; you don't have to give away millions of dollars or start your own foundation to make a difference. In fact, small, mostly free acts of kindness improve the lives of others just as much, (if not more,) than grand gestures of giving. The added side benefit is it'll give your spirit a lift, building on the cycle of giving and receiving that is so powerful.

Just remember, this chapter is not a list of instructions, it's full of helpful suggestions. If reading it makes you feel guilty in some vital way, or like you're not doing enough, just tell your brain, *Thank you for sharing* and pick one thing to start. See how that makes you feel, and then pick another thing. Relax, Glammer. It's a marathon, not a sprint.

Little things you can do for others

Remember the 'random acts of kindness' movement? Let's bring it back into the limelight.

You can start a deliberate practice by setting a reminder on your phone, or a sticky note on your refrigerator, to get in the

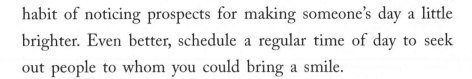

habit of noticing prospects for making someone's day a little brighter. Even better, schedule a regular time of day to seek out people to whom you could bring a smile.

Every random act of kindness starts with a simple question: *What can I do to give now?*

Yes, being NutriGlam is all about putting yourself first more often—and just as crucial is to remember to sometimes put others first, not because they expect it. Think about it: when were you last on the receiving end of a random act of kindness? Wouldn't it be awesome if that happened more often? You never know how many people you might inspire to do the same!

Here's a list of ideas to get you started:

1. If you see someone and notice how nice they look or how beautiful their smile is, tell them!

2. If you overhear someone else say something nice, pass that along to the person it was said about — like reverse gossip!

3. Make writing one nice note the first thing you do each day. Open your email inbox in the morning and write to the first person who comes to mind. The note can be as simple as, 'I just wanted to say thanks for being such a great friend,' or 'I'm thinking of you' or 'You'll

do great today!' Just 15 seconds can make someone's entire week.

4. As a family activity or a great idea for your next party, give each person a piece of paper with the name of every group member on the piece of paper. Tell each group member to write what you love about each person next to their name, then collect the papers, and write out the compliments anonymously on cards, presenting everyone with a card with their personal compliments.

5. Take five minutes to send a postcard to a sick child, member of the military serving overseas or even a prison inmate you don't know. You could make their day, spark a new friendship, or offer some much-needed relief.

6. On Mother's Day and Father's Day, remember your friends who have lost a parent, and check in with them. Those will be tough days and they will appreciate the gesture even if you just offer your presence.

7. Buy a few extra cans of soup or other non-perishables the next time you're grocery shopping and donate them to your local food bank.

8. Many animal shelters or veterinary hospitals accept donated pet food and gently used bedding items.

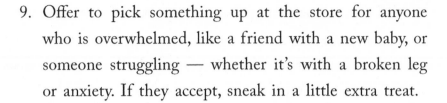

9. Offer to pick something up at the store for anyone who is overwhelmed, like a friend with a new baby, or someone struggling — whether it's with a broken leg or anxiety. If they accept, sneak in a little extra treat.

10. If you're an Amazon.com customer, you can donate Amazon's money to your favorite U.S. nonprofit through Amazon Smile. Amazon will donate to your favorite nonprofit each time you make a purchase. All you have to do is sign up and Amazon will even remind you each time to go through the proper portal, so they can give on your behalf.

11. If it's safe to do so, bring some flowers to the hospital for the nurses and doctors who work all day healing others.

12. Bring a healthy treat to work for everybody to share.

13. If you see a mom struggling with her kids at the supermarket, offer to get something off the shelf for her or help her to her car.

14. When everyone around you is gossiping about someone, be the one to butt in with something nice.

15. If you walk by a car with an expired parking meter, put money in it.

16. Take a person who just moved to town out on a personal tour.

17. Offer a homeless person a cup of coffee or take them to buy a meal. Giving them money may not suffice; a restaurant is more likely to allow them to make a purchase with you by their side.

18. Each time you get a new piece of clothing, donate an old one.

19. Write to an old teacher who made a difference in your life.

20. Leave a great waiter the biggest tip you can afford.

21. Let the next person have the parking space.

22. Bring your partner coffee (or breakfast) in bed.

23. Check in to ensure every person in a group conversation feels included and valued.

24. Send anonymous flowers to someone.

25. Pay the toll for the person behind you.

26. Leave some quarters in the laundromat.

27. Tithe your time — offer to do a chore for someone elderly, or take on a *pro bono* client a month.

28. Take in the neighbor's trash bins before they get home.

29. Contribute to the grocery bill of the person in line behind you.

30. Ask what supplies are most needed at your children's school, then buy them or take up a collection so that the school can buy them.

The power of human connection

Though social media is a fantastic invention for staying in touch and rediscovering long lost friends, nothing beats face-to-face conversation. Humans are communal creatures: we formed complex languages by observing one another and interacting to survive, so no wonder we feel lonely when we've not spoken to anyone in a while!

The next time you catch up with a friend via Facebook or WhatsApp, suggest meeting up for a coffee or—if they live further away—meeting at some destination in the middle for a day trip. Shopping, seeing the sights or even just enjoying a drink or lunch together is so different from hurried texts, and you'll have the added benefit of a new environment to keep the conversation lively. If it's not possible to meet in person, you can still use one of the many online apps such as Zoom, Skype or FaceTime to get some actual face time.

If you're more of an introvert Glammer, it's tough to know how to start having 'real life' conversations. That's fine—a

lot of people prefer a very small group of close-knit friends, maybe even just one or two, to large gatherings. Sometimes, more friends mean more drama, even if no Beautycons are involved... and who needs that?

Studies have proven that in-person conversations are good for your health, mental and physical.[24] Talking and interacting with someone you enjoy will lift your spirits and make you smile. They help you to open up and maybe share a few troubles to lighten the load—and you'll feel good when you listen to others.

Sometimes, it can be even simpler than that. Next time you're at the supermarket, just smile at another customer if they move aside to let you pass, or you catch their eye. Smile at a person you know you'll run into again, like the cashier or shelf-stocker. Make these little acknowledgements a part of your routine every time you go. If you're wearing a mask, you might exchange a couple of words instead—and that's enough. You've brightened their day, and your own, too.

I once started talking with a deli clerk at my neighborhood supermarket, and it turned out she fed and neutered all the stray cats that lived in the store parking lot. She paid for every one of their meals herself unless someone donated. I gave her some money and she started to cry. She hadn't known how she was going to spay a cat who had just shown up, and this would cover the fee at the low-cost clinic. I'm not sure who got more out of that exchange — let's just say we were both really happy we had connected.

How to give to charity

If you have a little extra and want to share it with a worthy cause, that's a terrific thing every Glammer should consider. Even a few dollars a month will make a difference.

Start by carefully choosing the cause you want to support; don't be pressured into it just because a representative caught you on the street or you got an email. It should involve an issue very close to your heart, like a problem you want to see eliminated or a smart idea you think should be more widely known.

Once you identify your cause or causes, don't feel guilty turning down all the others — it's your money, and other folks are donating to those worthy charities. Also, please watch for charity scams. You can look up a company online, even if they are standing right in front of you or on the phone, and make sure they are an actual charity and worthy of your contribution.

I once got a call from a VERY authoritative-sounding person, asking me to donate to the police, and insisting that I do so

on the call. He practically shouted down the line that it was my duty as an American. Since my spidey-sense was tingling, I did a quick online search, to discover that he was part of a right-wing political action group that had a deliberately deceptive name. Talk about a Beautycon!

If you have no money to spare, it's still easy to give to charity. Consider donating your unwanted belongings to places like Goodwill, or hold a garage or bake sale and donate the profits. Your local food bank or homeless shelter will appreciate items that are undamaged and in-date, just check with them beforehand so you can donate what they need most.

In some ways, your time is even more valuable than money. If you can spare even a couple of hours a week to help out a local soup kitchen program or animal shelter, you'll help keep these places open for the people who use and rely on them. You don't even need to find a charity—consider visiting an assisted living home to read, play games or just talk with the occupants. Or ask to visit a children's hospital in a superhero costume. You never know, you could have even more fun than the people you're entertaining!

Consider connecting restaurants or grocery stores with the homeless or homeless shelters. Did you know that according to the United Nations' Food and Agricultural Organization, "Food losses and waste amounts to roughly $680 billion

in industrialized countries and $310 billion in developing countries." [25]   In other words, we as a planet don't have a food shortage, we have an inappropriate allocation of resources.   Often because we don't have folks willing to connect those resources to a solution.

Homelessness is a chronic problem in the US and elsewhere across the globe, and it's particularly sad when you consider how many dilapidated old houses you see lying empty, or families missing loved ones who may have fallen on hard times. Homelessness is hard on everyone, yet it may be within our power to help.

If you see a person you see sleeping outside who may be in need of aid, alert charities or your local homeless shelter or even a church. Beware of giving spare change, as so often the homeless are victims of substance abuse; instead, bring them hot drinks or food, sit with them, and offer a few minutes of conversation. You'll be surprised at how many stories are out there.

You might be aware of the guerrilla knitting movement, which 'yarn-bombs' public spaces with charming acts of 3D art: garbage bin hats, for example, or colorful covers for abandoned bicycles. Some kind knitters have taken to tying hats, socks and mittens to lampposts in the winter with a note to homeless people inviting them to take whatever they need. Of course, if you have spare blankets, sleeping bags or warm

items of clothing, your local homeless shelter will be grateful for anything clean in good condition.

If you love knitting, crochet, patchwork or quilting, please consider making blankets for animal charities. Usually underfunded, these places can be very expensive to heat in the winter, and often sick or elderly animals are put up for adoption who need a little extra warmth. Most materials will be considered as long as the blankets are in good condition and freshly washed.

Here's a list of excellent charities to consider making your contributions[26] (all U.S dollar amounts accurate at time of publishing):

1. Scholarship America — provides college scholarships and financial aid to US students, and also help grassroots groups in setting up their own programs. It's awarded more than $2.9 billion to 1.9 million students, spending a whopping 97% of its total budget on its students. For example, a $50 donation buys an annual bus pass so that a community-college student can commute to campus.

2. Action Against Hunger — feeds malnourished children around the world while helping struggling communities grow their own food. They fulfill the mission by delivering aid to seven million people in more than 40

countries annually, and have taught over 43,000 people how to establish vegetable gardens and plant drought-resistant crops. A $45 donation provides 45 days of energy-dense food for a severely malnourished child.

3. Conservation International — helps protect the Earth and preserve healthy oceans, fresh water, and a stable climate. Operating fieldwork in over 40 countries, they study how economic and human development impacts

our tropical rainforests, grasslands, watersheds, and the sea. A $15 donation helps protect an acre of rainforest.

4. Save the Children — aims to eliminate poverty, disease, illiteracy, and hunger for children all over the world. They deliver direct assistance such as food and medicine, and access to education and financial tools, like savings programs that teach families how to put money aside for the future. A $70 donation provides education to a girl in Afghanistan for one year, including school fees, uniforms, books, and other supplies.

5. Humane Society of the United States — cares for animals and protects them from cruelty. They also offer vital services like free spaying and neutering, medical treatment, rescue and emergency care. A $100 donation provides an abused animal with medical care and shelter while it awaits adoption.

There are many others, including: Black Lives Matter, which explains: "By combating and countering acts of violence, creating space for Black imagination and innovation, and centering Black joy, we are winning immediate improvements in our lives."; Heifer International, which buys farm animals for villages to both sustainably feed and empower them; charity:water, which provides clean drinking water to those without it around the globe; Greenpeace, which helps fight

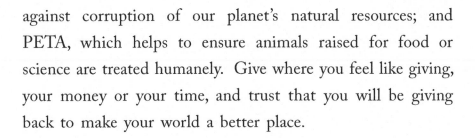

against corruption of our planet's natural resources; and PETA, which helps to ensure animals raised for food or science are treated humanely. Give where you feel like giving, your money or your time, and trust that you will be giving back to make your world a better place.

Volunteering is an act of self-care

Giving a little of ourselves is one of our highest callings. It makes others feel good, it gives us the warm fuzzies, and it helps advance our society and the whole human race. When every person does their bit to help someone else get a little further in life, we all progress faster, together.

Giving back also allows us to impact our community, connecting with local causes and people we would otherwise never have met. By volunteering in community gardens, beach cleans and kids' sport activities, we can make our neighborhood a better place to live—we can make a real difference.

Depending on what you choose to do, volunteering can help make you fitter and stronger by getting outdoors and doing some hard work. You'll also make new friends, expand your network, and boost your social skills.

Even better, it's good for our happiness chemistry. When researchers at the London School of Economics examined the relationship between volunteering and levels of happiness, they discovered that the more people volunteered, the happier they were. [27] Compared with people who never volunteered, the odds of being 'very happy' rose 7% among those who volunteered monthly and 12% for people who volunteered every two to four weeks. Among weekly volunteers, 16% felt very happy—an increase in overall levels of happiness comparable to having your income increased from $20,000 to $100,000. Abundance comes in many forms.

Working with animals has also been proven to have a beneficial effect on the brain. [27,28] Volunteering at an animal shelter or a riding stable, or even just walking your elderly neighbor's dogs, can boost your mood.

If you need a little extra persuading, consider this: volunteering is also excellent for your resume. Employers seek workers with a rounded life who know the benefits of working as a team and helping others, and if you can find a charity or volunteer program related to your dream job, you might find yourself top of the pile. Basically, it's NutriGlamorous!

Overall, helping out wherever and whenever we can gives us renewed purpose and a sense of greater meaning in life. If you're a Glammer who has retired or lost a spouse or partner, and you're looking for a new direction, you can find it in

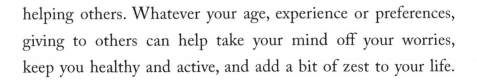

helping others. Whatever your age, experience or preferences, giving to others can help take your mind off your worries, keep you healthy and active, and add a bit of zest to your life.

More ways to give

There are many more ways to give back! Sometimes, the littlest things you can think of will create a chain reaction that makes everyone's day a bit more NutriGlam.

Giving is all about making the world a better place: for you, and for others. This book is way too short for all the brilliant ideas out there, so here are fifty small ways to help you give. Why not make a game of it and see how many you, or your family, can complete?

1. If you buy something from a charity, pay double.

2. Buy your utilities from suppliers who use sustainable resources.

3. Pay compliments (all the time).

4. Tell someone their clothes label is sticking out (even if you don't know them).

5. Bring birds into your garden: Get or build a bird feeder, and make sure your cat has a bell on its collar.

6. If you're buying a new car, consider new zero-emission vehicles.

7. If you don't have a low-flow toilet already, put a brick in the tank to reduce the amount of water used in flushing.

8. Give your old computer or laptop to someone in the developing world or an underprivileged child.

9. If you win cash, donate a portion to charity.

10. Take action on things you find badly run or offensive. Make your voice heard. Participate. Get organized and address the issue — don't just let it be someone else's problem.

11. Throw a street party and get to know your neighbors.

12. Join a team sport (maybe instead of the gym).

13. Register as an organ donor.

14. Paint the outside of your house to brighten up your street.

15. Support your local businesses — buy from small Mom n' Pop stores. (Can't get there now? Buy gift certificates for later.)

16. If you have the choice, travel by train, not plane.

17. Pay to carbon offset your plane travel.

18. Encourage children to become leaders and teach them to care for others.

19. Write your local congressperson to lobby an issue, or just to say you appreciate what a great job she's doing.

20. Plant green plants in window boxes on the street-side of your home to help combat car pollution.

21. Plant flowers in your front yard or in potholes and cracks to cheer up the road.

22. Learn a couple great jokes so you can make people laugh.

23. Always make eye contact and don't crouch when talking to someone in a wheelchair.

24. Offer your arm to an elderly or blind person at a crosswalk.

25. Take a first aid course so you can use it when you need to.

26. Give blood as often as you can.

27. Keep an eye on your elderly neighbors. Watch for signs of distress, changes in their behavior or chores you can offer help with.

28. Always give a tip.

29. Keep a bowl of fruit on your desk at work and encourage others to help themselves.

30. Find out the names of the chefs, security guards, cleaners and staff who serve you, and say their names when you speak with them; you'd be surprised how rarely that happens.

31. If you see someone lost, take out your phone and look up directions together.

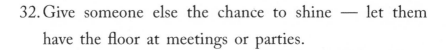

32. Give someone else the chance to shine — let them have the floor at meetings or parties.

33. Tell someone they did a good job. Better yet, tell their boss.

34. Create art. Share it with the world: or just one special person.

35. Spend some uninterrupted time with a child. Give them 100% of your attention.

36. Slip a $5 bill or a handwritten note of encouragement into a library book.

37. Mentor or coach someone who wants to learn from you.

38. Give someone you love a hug for no reason other than you care.

39. Give someone a book you've read and enjoyed.

40. Leave books in public places like bus terminals and gas stations for others to find.

41. Connect two people who would enjoy each other's friendship.

42. Turn off lights when you leave a room.

43. Turn off the water while you brush your teeth.

44. Unplug your devices when not in use.

45. Adopt a rescue pet.

46. Carry a protein bar in your bag, and give it to a homeless person.

47. Put someone who has had too much to drink in a cab.

48. Take an electricity-free day and shut everything down.

49. Offer to run an errand for a neighbor who is ill.

50. Smile more. Smile often.

Think about this: we can give just by being good humans, bettering ourselves internally and externally, showing up as considerate, polite people in the face of an increasingly unkind society. Here are fifty ways for you to live that will make you even more NutriGlamorous:

1. Carry stress balls to squeeze when you feel under pressure.

2. Ride on the swings in the kids' park.

3. Fold the laundry properly, instead of using the clean clothes basket as an extra closet.

4. Listen to rain, or ocean waves, or rainforest noises.

5. Turn off your phone notifications at dinner time and leave the phone in another room.

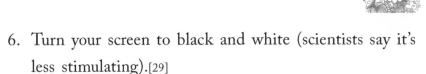

6. Turn your screen to black and white (scientists say it's less stimulating).[29]

7. Understand your privilege. If it's not your skin color, religion or history, learn about it and don't presume you have any idea what it feels like inside.

8. Go out and experience the world.

9. Write down the number of mistakes you make in one day, and aim to double it. It's a great way to learn!

10. Switch off your phone before going into a public event.

11. Create a gratitude journal. Write down what you're grateful for, every single day.

12. Look out for the first colorful leaves of fall, or blossoms of spring.

13. Listen to the radio and sing along.

14. Learn to love the smell of fresh ironing.

15. Share a podcast or YouTube subscription that uplifts you (and listen to it often).

16. Get kids together to watch a movie you loved as a child.

17. Stretch your mind (and your body) daily, and share your new knowledge.

18. Look up at the stars more often. Get to know the planets and constellations.

19. Take a trip out to the countryside and be still: listen to the quiet.

20. Light a scented candle or stick of incense.

21. Replace the toilet paper roll when it's empty.

22. Always write thank-you letters.

23. Listen to songs that make you feel at one with the world — such as John Lennon's *Imagine*, or Bette Midler or Nancy Griffiths' covers of *From a Distance*.

24. Vote. Exercise your right to democracy. Every time. People died so you could.

25. Educate yourself. Learn about other cultures, faiths, ideas, languages, people and histories.

26. When you visit museums and galleries, buy from their cafes and gift shops, too.

27. Take time away from others when you're ill; you're not doing anyone a favor by "powering through" and you might get everyone around you sick, too.

28. Travel respectfully: Don't block aisles, pack your luggage properly, realize people are behind you — so don't stop to check your phone.

29. Get more sleep.

30. Get rid of clutter.

31. Improve your posture with yoga.

32. Drive sensibly.

33. Wrap used baby wipes, tampons or sanitary napkins and put them in the trash, not the toilet. In third world countries, put any toilet paper in the trash, too.

34. Always take responsibility for your situation, good or bad; blame is for Beautycons.

35. Say YES more.

36. Pledge to be more honest.

37. Learn a new language.

38. Do at least one cultural thing a week.

39. Get to know more about where you live. Research local property information, crime rates, politics and history.

40. Wear bright clothes at least once a week. It will cheer everyone up — especially you!

41. Have your ticket/documents/forms out and ready before you get to the usher/inspector/clerk.

42. Don't talk in a theatre and don't pull out your cell phone in the dark.

43. Carry mints and visit your dentist; bad breath can be a sign of bad health.

44. Dog owners: pick up that poop, always!

45. Don't push.

46. Don't yell at kids. Especially not your own. You're bigger than that, Glammer. Remember, they installed your buttons — that's why they push them.

47. Devote your attention to a loved one's company.

48. Take an offline day, a "Technology Shabbat" and shut off all those electronics.

49. Take a deep breath and count to three before responding to an argumentative comment.

50. Spend time in a garden, whether weeding, planting, or strolling.

Enjoy doing a few of these, or even trying all of them to see which ones fit you best. You're on your way to being even more Nutriglam.

"Tell the truth, or someone will tell it for you."

— Stephanie Klein

Truth

I t's time to be honest with yourself.

Becoming NutriGlamorous is all about the truth with a capital T, facing up to things we can't change, don't actually want to change or really need to change, as well as the things that are actually perfect the way they are.

That's why the Beautycon myth is so persuasive. It acts as an emergency exit out of the really tough stuff life throws into our path: growth, love, change and confrontation. When you get to the other side of those tough things, that's what makes life worth living.

Discovering your truth isn't just one step to becoming a Glammer; it's the underlying philosophy of being NutriGlam. Beautycons have been misled into thinking they need a brand-new mask with every passing trend and that they aren't good enough unless they fit others' opinions on who and what they should be. They're constantly frightened, sad, lonely, or unhappy with who they are. Most of them just need a hug!

To be a Glammer, you must step into your Truth: whatever it may be. It's about saying, "I won't attempt to match up to anyone's expectations—even my own." Instead of shoving yourself into a mold (even one of your own creation), allow your soul to settle into the shape it fits naturally.

Your NutriGlamorous truth is distilled from your past experiences, present situation, and future dreams—maybe not what you wish you had, just your real world today as you know it.

I like to say, everything is just a Grand Experiment. So when you are living your Truth, if you don't like something, you can always change it or do something you like better. Enjoy the experiment! Live as full out as you can.

How do you find your truth? First, give yourself permission to try out things you've never done before, maybe because you didn't think you had enough time, or you'd look silly, or it was too late, or whatever reason (i.e., excuse!) you told yourself.

Consider the experience afterwards. Did you find it lived up to your expectations? Was it more fun or rewarding, or less scary, or as pointless as you thought? Did you smile because everyone else was expecting you to? Or did it something different than you were expecting?

Whatever your opinion, the third step is to simply let the experience naturally settle into your life. If you want to do it again, go for it—or consciously observe what's stopping you (Guilt? Time constraints? Money?) and eliminate the problem if you are able. If you'd be happy either way, let it go—don't let anyone pressure you—and if you didn't like the experience, be brave enough to admit this to yourself and don't let anyone or anything make you do it again. This is harder than it looks. You've got this, Glammer—this is how you discover your Truth.

Apply this practice to every area of your life, in your smallest actions and reactions, and things will start moving into a better place. Beautycons will find you much less interesting, you'll naturally find more time for yourself, you may get

a whole new circle of friends, and you'll become happier, more fulfilled, and more YOU.

Of course, the current situation, the one that looks like the "truth" is sometimes ugly. We're not yet who we want to be, or we can't seem to get happy with our bodies, or in our current jobs. Nothing can fall into place because there are too many factors to wrestle with, or it all seems out of our control.

When this happens, it's time to do some heavy lifting.

Bravery is the first and most essential part of this process: it's how you face up to your challenges. Don't fear being 'average.' Average is its own kind of special because everyone contributes in their own way.

Instead, shun the Beautycon way of life—constantly hunted by invisible enemies that live inside their own heads, unable to admit even what they want to wear or what they truly want for dinner...

When you live your Truth, you will finally hush all the negative voices in your head. They have nothing to say to you when you are living the life of your dreams. Sometimes it's chocolate cake, and sometimes it's organic veggie juice.

Get it, Glammer? Balance.

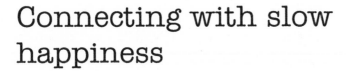

Connecting with slow happiness

Let's say you're feeling unmotivated, unsure of yourself, a bit listless, not really sure what your purpose in life is—being a Glammer is all well and good, you say, it's just... how?

Do an online search, and you'll find a million articles online telling you how to find your purpose. While these are all possibilities, to find YOUR truth, you will have to examine your own life with open eyes and a clear heart.

Because it's more than likely you already have inspiration, and a purpose. You just might not be doing or feeling these things often enough in your life, so you need to address the balance.

Happiness comes in many forms. The giddy, rollercoaster, honeymoon-type happiness is big, and loud, and noticeable. This kind of experience—like a promotion at work, a glittering romance, or a treasured purchase—is the sprinkles on the cupcake. The foundation of being NutriGlamorous is solid, sweetly nourishing contentment—a quiet, everyday happiness.

Because the truth is that happiness is stable, sustainable, within our reach, and will impact our lives and communities in powerful ways if we will allow it.

So to find that kind of happiness and cultivate more, you want to keep moving towards that which makes you happy.

The truth with a capital T

You want the real Truth?

Here it is: becoming a Glammer is your life's work. Just as it's your life's work to be in joy, to make the best choices for you, and to keep moving towards the things that make you happy.

These can be powerful changes, especially if you've been negative for a long time. No fad diets, no spring trends whizzing by. It's the foundation for a whole new 'you-ier' you. And it starts today with you making a commitment to yourself.

If this is your first time making these changes, you may get into arguments with your family, cause your spouse to worry about or resent you changing, butt heads at work or even decide to take a different career path. You might not like eating healthier at first, and you already don't feel like you have time for everything you want to do.

Here's a simple mantra for you: I'm growing.

Remember why you're doing it: healthful changes, a happier life. Authenticity, and being a better person for you and everyone around you.

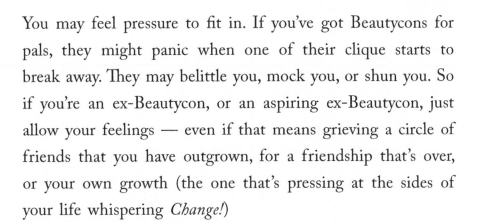

You may feel pressure to fit in. If you've got Beautycons for pals, they might panic when one of their clique starts to break away. They may belittle you, mock you, or shun you. So if you're an ex-Beautycon, or an aspiring ex-Beautycon, just allow your feelings — even if that means grieving a circle of friends that you have outgrown, for a friendship that's over, or your own growth (the one that's pressing at the sides of your life whispering *Change!*)

Remember to approach friendships and break-ups with an open mind and forgiving nature, just like you're treating yourself now. True friendships will survive—and you might rescue a couple of Beautycons at the same time!

You may also see a return to old behavior for a while — your pendulum swinging from one extreme to another. That's okay, too. Honor your process of growing and allow better things to flow back into your life.

Asking for Help

How many times have you said to a friend or relative in need, "Let me know if there's anything I can do to help," and truly meant it? You'd jump at the chance to feel useful in a bad situation, make them feel special and take a load off their shoulders. So why are we so bad at accepting help?

The truth is, helping someone in need is a gift from the person in need to the helper: it's saying, "I trust you, you are useful, and I need you in my life right now." People feel helpless when others are experiencing difficulties: though you can't mend broken legs, undo grief or provide winning lottery tickets, if you can do just a little to brighten a cloudy day, you and the receiver both feel better.

So remember that, Glammer — who are you to deny others the pleasure of helping you?

The best way to ask for help is to banish the thought you might be bossy, bothering someone, or a burden. Then, ask someone you trust, and who has the capacity to help in the situation you need. Give them a specific task to do: people aren't mind readers, and they might tend to bring flowers or a candle, when what someone who's sick or overwhelmed really needs is a few errands run or a healthy lunch.

If this feels impossible for you, it's likely associated with your childhood — a fear of asking for help because perhaps there was none available to you then. Ask yourself, "What's the worst thing that will happen?" Chances are, it will be as simple as being afraid of rejection, which everyone feels sometimes! Any fear can be overcome once you realize that's what's holding you back. You know the bumper sticker: Feel the fear and do it anyway! You're not getting the result you

want now, so why not ask for the help you need? If they do say no, you'll be no worse off than you are now.

How to ditch old, bad habits

Got a bad habit you want to get rid of? Maybe you smoke, snack too much or grind your teeth.

Well, most bad habits are caused by two things: stress and boredom.

Everything from drinking too much on a weekend to overspending and biting our nails can be our own unique process of handling unpleasant sensations. Of course, this means we can treat the causes of stress and boredom or just identify our triggers so we can replace our bad habits with healthier ones.

In some ways, bad habits are actually benefiting you— otherwise you'd never do them at all. [31] That simple, tiny rush of serotonin you get is enough to create a lifetime habit. You may feel more connected to friends if you constantly check Facebook, even though you see more bad news than good and it's killing your productivity. Or, your inner perfectionist may be satisfied if you chew away tiny pieces of your cuticles.

This is why it's useless to say 'just stop it'; you rely on these little hits to power you through your day.

You can choose a substitute for your bad habit, which involves logical thinking and planning ahead, so only go down this route if you have the time and space in your life to tackle it. For example, if you feel like you want a cigarette, you can try breathing mindfully for five minutes or having a healthy snack instead.

If you have limited resources to prep and plan for your bad habits, change your environment to eliminate as many triggers as possible. If you're a social drinker, meet up with friends in the park or on a hike. If you struggle to get up with the alarm, place it on the other side of the room so you have to get out of bed (and don't let Alexa be your alarm clock).

Or, invite some accountability in your life. Does a friend want to break a bad habit as well? A healthy-eating meetup may work for you because they offer a sense of community, a shared goal and a support network: someone to cheer for you when you succeed, and buck you up when you hit setbacks. You might do something public, like announce your bad habit on social media and use the comment section as your accountability, or make a promise to treat yourself if you can resist your bad habit for 30 days.

You weren't born with your bad habits; they aren't your Glammer truth unless you accept them as your truth. Just as they're learned, they can be unlearned, often in less time it took to acquire those habits in the first place. Even if it was years ago, you once lived without this way of behaving, so you can definitely do it again.

Growing into yourself

Let's tackle a core issue here, Glammer—what does it really mean to be yourself?

We often use it as a shortcut—even in this book—when what we really mean is: moving into a higher state of understanding about what we choose to be aligned with; living authentically, moment to moment.

People (yes, mostly Beautycons) can corrupt the concept of being yourself. They use it as an excuse for bad behavior ("I'm just being me!"), or put you down ("Stop being fake!") What's going on?

Truthfully, we're all being ourselves, all the time—so we need to start saying what we mean. This is difficult, because it means having the awareness to tell someone, "I don't like who you're becoming," or, "I miss the old way you used to joke with me," or, "I think you're trying too hard and it's uncomfortable." That's not easy to say, or hear.

If anyone says you aren't yourself, or that you should stop doing something because it doesn't fit their idea of you, when you're genuinely happy and comfortable doing it—and you aren't harming others, of course—feel free to tell them where to go.

Let's talk about what this means for your body.

Lash extensions, plastic surgery, fillers and other cosmetic enhancements are typically thought to be exclusive Beautycon pursuits: after all, if you want to change your body into something it's not in that moment, isn't that being fake and untrue to your real self?

Absolutely not, Glammer, if you're doing it for you. Simple example: get the boob job because it will make YOU happy, not because you think your husband will stop staring at other women or because he's pressuring you into it.

Dolly Parton LOVES her breasts, and she makes sure the world knows about it. Is she less of an authentic person because she's chosen a path that she thinks is the best one for her? The woman is over three-quarters of a century old, and she loves the way she looks. That's what you want for yourself, and whether you disagree with Dolly's choices, that woman is a Glammer through and through — authentic to herself, and not caring one bit what the rest of the world thinks about it. She also has contributed millions of dollars to children's literacy, and paid to rebuild her entire home town after a disaster struck, so her heart is even bigger than her ta-tas.

The same goes for nutritional supplements, stimulants or calmatives, as long as you're not using them to excess or harming yourself. It would be great if we could get 110% of our nutrients in a balanced diet, get enough sleep and be energized at work; it just doesn't work that way all the time.[30] You aren't 'giving up' or becoming a Beautycon if you choose to ingest something that isn't organic or a whole food — choose what works for you.

If you think about it, we're constantly changing our bodies outside as well as inside, in response to our environment, needs, and our whims and desires.

Tattoos are body modifications, and so is losing weight. Plucking your eyebrows, getting a leg wax, fitting a prosthetic,

even styling your hair are all forms of body modification. If we all decided to go *au natural* from birth, the world would be a different place (more interesting, to say the least).

One of the arguments against body modification has to do with permanence. Waxing hair and wearing high heels doesn't last. A nose job or a tattoo is forever! There's a joke about archaeologists of the future digging up supermodels with strange plastic sponges in their chests.

Who really cares? In a world where we're still expected to choose our careers at fifteen, where we can get pregnant at sixteen and vote at eighteen, our actions have way more permanent and far-reaching consequences than how we choose to decorate our skin.

Besides, in an age of relentless consumerism and fast-paced trends, it's empowering to take back our own time and decide to create something that will last years.

Body modification, in essence, is changing our outsides to match our insides. Don't let anyone tell you your body isn't a gift, a blank canvas on which to display the beauty you wish to show to the world. Whether you're honoring a higher power by getting a religious tattoo or growing your hair a certain way, or whether you want to look sexy, hip or rebellious, or whether your journey is showing the world your true gender or ability—your body is yours.

"*The things you are passionate about are not random. They are your calling.*"

— Fabienne Fredrickson

Next

This book has all the delicious tools you need to start your journey of becoming NutriGlamorous.

You have a rewarding experience ahead of you— being a Glammer is a lifetime occupation that you are more than ready for!

You already know that being NutriGlam is all about moving into your truth and becoming your authentic, beautiful, life-loving self— while side-stepping negative influences, treating yourself with love, and showing up with optimism in your heart.

It's all about making room for more of what you love, thinking about the things you don't like so much in new ways, and discovering new ideas, dreams and activities to ignite your joy and imagination. It's also about allowing ourselves to be brave and kind: to lower our defenses and take care of ourselves, so we have overflowing joy to give to others.

You also now know how to spot a Beautycon, and why that lifestyle isn't all it's cracked up to be.

Above all, you now know that there is no perfect blueprint; have fun just creating your own. Whether your idea of NutriGlamorous involves protein powder, supplements and weightlifting, or walking through the park, listening to audiobooks and chai tea, or drinks in the yard as you enjoy your kids playing on the slip n' slide—there is no wrong way

to be a Glammer, as long as you're honest with yourself and those you love.

How to move forward

Every day we make choices, large and small. Those choices add up to who we are, shape who we want to be, and influence

who we will become. Whether it's what you're cooking for dinner or what you say to a wrong number, you have literally thousands of chances every day to define your version of NutriGlam.

Being a Glammer begins with one small, very important, choice: for the first few weeks, resolve to change absolutely nothing. Instead, simply observe; get a picture of who you are.

Live your life like a painter studying her subject: what's happening? How are you reacting? How do you handle the unexpected? Are you aware of most decisions? What do you find annoying, charming, funny or worrying? Don't try to change the course of your thoughts, like rerouting a river. Just let it flow.

Without making any judgments, gauge the current state of your life—and then sit down, and think about the kind of life you'd really like and the person you want to be. Is she similar to your present experience? Do you only need to make a couple changes? Or does your NutriGlam you seem like an insurmountable challenge?

Only when we start to adjust our sails does the wind seem to blow in our favor. Though you may have thought you knew what you want from life, now you might go back to your plans and change a few priorities — it's always a good time

to take stock of both your blessings and what you may want to alter.

Without mindful direction and purpose, without setting your intentions for your own desires, you are vulnerable to being molded by outside forces, people and stimuli. This can leave you with a vague sense of unease, even if everything's okay right now. When you know you can shape your future, and you're taking steps to get better at doing so, it gives you a deep-rooted sense of power and shores up your purpose.

Realizing you're living a life you don't truly love can make you feel like you're just going through the paces, or perhaps that your life is actually meaningless. It happens when you don't act with purpose or fail to be mindful of your reactions and habits. It's easy enough to fall into the Beautycon trap by not paying attention, or paying too much to the wrong things.

What if, on your NutriGlamorous journey, you realize you want to choose new things and start living a new way — that although things are unsustainable as they are, you have absolutely no idea what the life you want looks like? How do you find an answer to a question you can't put into words?

Find role models

A great place to start is to gather around you those people you admire. Make a list of the people you look up to most, and why you admire them.

Even though we're born with two parents, most of us get to have more—as other, possibly wiser, role models show up in our lives. Being conscious of this process allows you to seek mentorship in others, and open your eyes to new ways of learning, like you did when you were a child.

Who do you look up to? Your answer belongs just to you—you could select the woman at the local bookshop, the girl on Instagram who you only know by her @, your neighbor, a friend, an ancestor, a TV host, a vet—anyone.

Here's an easy exercise that can help you get clarity for yourself: write one small phrase, even just a word, about what you admire about them. It can be tempting to put others on pedestals and make them into perfect beings. Instead, treat this list like a smorgasbord, picking and choosing your favorite qualities — this is the self to which you choose to aspire.

It might be the way they style their clothes, or that they seem jubilant all the time. It could be their lightning wit, ability to captivate a room, their way with animals or that they know

all the yoga poses. They could be dynamic and career-driven, or mellow and holistic.

Finally, the most important part of this exercise: what are the tiniest steps you can take, right now, towards becoming more of what you admire in these people? If you want to lose weight, your goal might be simply to drink one extra glass of water. It's really okay if it's that small. If you want to be rich, start by setting up a savings plan (even if it's just $10

a week!) or if you want to start a yoga practice, then look up one asana online.

Take one small step, right now, and trust that you are already on your way.

What's Next

There are a ton of places you can go to expand your knowledge as you continue your NutriGlam journey—many of them are online (you'll find excellent resources in the References section at the end of this book).

As a general rule, your immediate circle is a great place to start. Not only will your tribe give you personal attention, they are more likely to actually care about you and your well-being. Often your closest and most trusted friends are able to pick up on signs you've lost your way—and help you get back on track. Your inner circle is immediately accessible, a great place to start when you're looking for accountability, new ideas and insight into habits you may want to change.

Of course, blindly trusting your friends and family, especially when it comes to the tricky subject of self-growth, may not be the best course for your NutriGlamorous self. They could

be struggling with the same problems, be confused about (and possibly reject) your Glammer habits, or be closeted Beautycons with their own agenda, which, in an attempt to protect themselves, might include sabotaging you. Use your intuition and discernment here.

Check out the unlimited wealth of published information on the subject of self-improvement. Much of the information you are looking for can be found with a quick online search, and don't underestimate the power of holding a physical book. Go to Amazon or your local library or bookstore, starting with self-help, healthy eating, spirituality and philosophy — the foundations of a well-rounded Glammer.

Next, consider joining a self-help retreat or seminar if you have a particular topic to tackle such as emotional intelligence, weight loss, or removing energy blocks. Being in a room with a group of people on your exact personal mission is an extremely powerful motivator, and you'll get an extra boost helping out your fellow attendees.

Another hugely important resource is, of course, the professional. Coaches, therapists and counsellors can help you survive and tackle the challenges that come your way. Treat them as mechanics, and you're the car! The last thing you want is to break down completely and have to be pushed into a garage, so pay attention to the importance of a regular tune-up.

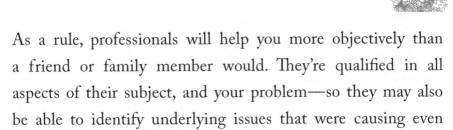

As a rule, professionals will help you more objectively than a friend or family member would. They're qualified in all aspects of their subject, and your problem—so they may also be able to identify underlying issues that were causing even more damage than you realized.

Working with a professional is never easy, and your first challenge is finding the right fit for you. You need to find the right specialist (i.e., personal coach, business coach, therapist) and then interview the ones who resonate with you to find the best fit.

If you feel there's a stigma in seeking their help, just say "thank you for sharing" to your brain and move forward. If anyone makes you feel that way, they're probably a Beautycon—because a Glammer knows when to ask for help when she needs it, and isn't afraid to explore what's inside herself. Relax and do what you need to do for yourself.

Other resources include spiritual leaders, psychics, doctors, personal trainers, professional organizations and charities. Ask all the questions until you feel comfortable, allowing yourself to follow your heart and your own inquisitive nature.

A message of love and resilience

You are amazing, Glammer! You already have all you need to get on the road to becoming your best self.

Remember to always treat yourself with kindness, give yourself a break, and let yourself slip up once in a while. No one's perfect!

Use all the tools available to you to lift your spirits, grow your dreams, and unblock you so you can succeed even beyond those dreams. This path is allows you to enjoy your life — to love the present, and love who you are! The real pleasure, as the bumper sticker says, is in the journey, not the destination. It's there we make our most important discoveries.

And remember, you were never meant to be a superwoman, dashing from place to place, saving everyone, having it all and being everything at once—you are simply here to have a happy life full of health, love and laughter, whatever that means to you.

No more, no less, than a life that's totally NutriGlamorous.

References

1. Ward EM, MS, RD. Personalize Your Diet Plan: How to Design a Diet around Your Eating Habits. In: WebMD [Internet]. [cited 29 Sep 2017]. Available: http://www.webmd.com/diet/features/how-to-design-your-own-diet

2. ShapeFit. Calories Per Day Calculator — How Many Calories Do You Need? In: ShapeFit.com [Internet]. 4 Apr 2015 [cited 29 Sep 2017]. Available: https://www.shapefit.com/calculators/calories-per-day-calculator.html

3. Schwenk TL. Alternate-Day Fasting Is No Better Than a Typical Reduced-Calorie Diet. NEJM Journal Watch. Journal Watch; 2017;2017: NA44082.

4. Gibson A. Easy Guide to Growing Microgreens — The Micro Gardener. In: The Micro Gardener [Internet]. 10 Mar 2013 [cited 29 Sep 2017]. Available: https://themicrogardener.com/easy-guide-to-growing-microgreens/

5. Schumm, L. America's Patriotic Victory Gardens. In: History.com [Internet] Aug 18, 2018 https://www.history.com/news/americas-patriotic-victory-gardens

6. How to Determine Your PERFECT Workout Plan | Nerd Fitness. In: Nerd Fitness [Internet]. 16 May 2013 [cited 29 Sep 2017]. Available: https://www.

nerdfitness.com/blog/how-to-determine-your-perfect-workout-plan/

7. Wong K. Why Humans Give Birth to Helpless Babies. In: Scientific American Blog Network [Internet]. [cited 29 Sep 2017]. Available: https://blogs.scientificamerican.com/observations/why-humans-give-birth-to-helpless-babies/

8. Goldman K. If You Do Nothing Else For Exercise, Walk 10 Minutes A Day. In: mindbodygreen [Internet]. 2 Sep 2014 [cited 29 Sep 2017]. Available: http://www.mindbodygreen.com/0-15120/if-you-do-nothing-else-for-exercise-walk-10-minutes-a-day.html

9. Firman T. This Is How Many Calories You Burn From Walking. In: Dr Oz The Good Life [Internet]. 24 Aug 2016 [cited 29 Sep 2017]. Available: http://www.drozthegoodlife.com/fitness/a2225/calories-burned-from-walking/

10. Cherlynn Low LSW. How to Block Someone With Extreme Prejudice [Internet]. [cited 29 Sep 2017]. Available: https://www.laptopmag.com/articles/how-to-block

11. Inflammation in Fear- and Anxiety-Based Disorders: PTSD, GAD, and Beyond https://www.ncbi.nlm.nih.gov/pmc/articles/PMC5143487/

12. Spiritual Integrity: What Does it Mean to be Spiritual? In: Evolving Beings [Internet]. [cited 29 Sep 2017]. Available: http://www.evolvingbeings.com/post/spiritual-integrity-what-does-it-mean-to-be-spiritual

13. 11 Powerful Affirmations to Help Treat Depression and Anxiety. In: Power of Positivity: Positive Thinking & Attitude [Internet]. 23 Aug 2014 [cited 29 Sep 2017]. Available: https://www.powerofpositivity.com/11-powerful-affirmations-help-treat-depression-anxiety/

14. Yogitimes.com. What Is The Meaning Of Om. In: Yogi Times [Internet]. [cited 29 Sep 2017]. Available: https://www.yogitimes.com/article/what-is-om-mean-meaning-sanskrit

15. The Hidden Costs of Fossil Fuels. In: Union of Concerned Scientists [Internet]. [cited 29 Sep 2017]. Available: http://www.ucsusa.org/clean-energy/coal-and-other-fossil-fuels/hidden-cost-of-fossils

16. Reusable vs. disposable nappies: which is better for the environment? | OVO Energy [Internet]. [cited 29 Sep 2017]. Available: https://www.ovoenergy.com/blog/green/reusable-vs-disposable-nappies-which-is-better-for-the-environment.html

17. Composting: a guide to making compost at home, using compost tumblers, bins & other composters

| Eartheasy.com [Internet]. [cited 29 Sep 2017]. Available: http://eartheasy.com/grow_compost.html

18. Tax Credits and Deductions to Help Your Business "Go Green." In: The Balance [Internet]. [cited 29 Sep 2017]. Available: https://www.thebalance.com/tax-credits-and-deductions-for-your-going-green-business-4052679

19. Make Do and Mend. Available: http://www.bl.uk/index.shtml

20. Blay Z, 16 Books About Race That Every White Person Should Read. In: The Huffington Post. [cited 29 Sep 2017]. Available: https://www.huffpost.com/entry/16-books-about-race-that-every-white-person-should-read_n_565f37e8e4b08e945fedaf49

21. Twitter [Internet]. [cited 29 Sep 2017]. Available: https://twitter.com/editoremilye/status/797243415922515970?ref_src=twsrc%5Etfw

22. Women's rights in Saudi Arabia https://en.wikipedia.org/wiki/Women%27s_rights_in_Saudi_Arabia

23. Morrison K. Survey: 92% of Recruiters Use Social Media to Find High-Quality Candidates. In: Adweek [Internet]. 22 Sep 2015 [cited 29 Sep 2017]. Available: http://www.adweek.com/digital/survey-96-of-recruiters-use-social-media-to-find-high-quality-candidates/

24. Evans L. Why You Need To Actually Talk To Your Coworkers Face To Face. In: Fast Company [Internet]. Fast Company; 13 Oct 2014 [cited 29 Sep 2017]. Available: https://www.fastcompany.com/3036935/why-you-need-to-actually-talk-to-your-coworkers-face-to-face

25. SAVE FOOD: Global Initiative on Food Loss and Waste Reduction http://www.fao.org/save-food/resources/keyfindings/en/

26. Tsui BB. A List of 10 Top Charities. In: Real Simple [Internet]. [cited 29 Sep 2017]. Available: https://www.realsimple.com/work-life/money/list-charities

27. Volunteering and its Surprising Benefits: How Giving to Others Makes You Healthier and Happier [Internet]. [cited 29 Sep 2017]. Available: https://www.helpguide.org/articles/healthy-living/volunteering-and-its-surprising-benefits.htm

28. Beetz A, Uvnäs-Moberg K, Julius H, Kotrschal K. Psychosocial and Psychophysiological Effects of Human-Animal Interactions: The Possible Role of Oxytocin. Front Psychol. Frontiers Media SA; 2012;3. doi:10.3389/fpsyg.2012.00234

29. Hamblin J, Pollock N, Skurie J. To Break a Phone Addiction, Turn Your Screen Gray [Internet]. Available:

http://www.theatlantic.com/video/index/480240/
adventures-in-grayscale/

30. Should You Take Dietary Supplements? In: NIH
News in Health [Internet]. 30 May 2017 [cited
29 Sep 2017]. Available: https://newsinhealth.nih.
gov/2013/08/should-you-take-dietary-supplements

31. Clear J. How to Break a Bad Habit (and Replace It
With a Good One). In: James Clear [Internet]. 13 May
2013 [cited 29 Sep 2017]. Available: http://jamesclear.
com/how-to-break-a-bad-habit

Made in the USA
Coppell, TX
02 November 2020